Ready Aim Fire

Ready Aim Fire

Denise Flippen

Xulon Press

Xulon Press
2301 Lucien Way #415
Maitland, FL 32751
407.339.4217
www.xulonpress.com

© 2017 by . Denise Flippen

All rights reserved solely by the author. The author guarantees all contents are original and do not infringe upon the legal rights of any other person or work. No part of this book may be reproduced in any form without the permission of the author. The views expressed in this book are not necessarily those of the publisher.

Scripture quotations taken from the Holy Bible, New International Version (NIV). Copyright © 2011 by Biblica, Inc.™. Used by permission. All rights reserved.

Printed in the United States of America.

ISBN-13: 9781545606605

Utilizing the NIV translation of the Holy Bible, I will be comparing God's word to our current situations. This study is recommended as a group study guide to create dialog of the contents. The information is limited, as discussions amongst the group is highly encouraged to build intimate relationships, and to receive revelations from God Himself. This will help everyone to get to know one another while build supportive and accountability circles. Part 1 Love: The Effective Weapon is recommended as a daily 2-week study, but can be studied weekly as well. Parts, 2 Help: The Lifestyle of a Worshiper, and 3 Hello: Fasting from the Other Side are recommended as weekly studies.

Homework is limited to journaling. Reflecting on what have been discussed and seeking God to bring about the clarity, will assist you in bringing about necessary changes in your life. Journaling nightly will be beneficial, serving as a mirror. You will see where you fall short, and how God is moving in your life. This is the application phase. Share inserts from your journal with your group as you feel comfortable.

You may also utilize this study as an individual study. God's word is sufficient, but if possible grab a friend or two. It's nice to share ideas and revelations that the Lord will give you. We will discuss what a life of worship looks and feels like. There will be many challenging perspectives as we uncover many religious, and traditional views within Christianity. My pray is that with studying the word of God, that we may remove God from the limited box of our minds, and place Him in the sovereignty of our lives. God loves you all, and so do I. Enjoy!

INTRODUCTION

Ready Aim Fire… is a study guide designated to highlight key points pertaining to loving others in the midst of our current violate and fearful climate. Mask are being pulled off, and individuals hearts are being exposed. This is a difficult reality within the church. Christianity was supposed to be about people who were set free from darkness and captivity to set others free as well, being rooted in love. Things have switched, up and the heart of man has changed once again. We have gone from sharing the love of God, to teaching people to fear Him. Yes, hell is real, but many people are experiencing hell here on earth. There is a way to avoid hell that is being lived out on earth. Getting to know and experiencing a loving God through daily interaction with the body of Christ is a great start. We need to not only focus on holiness, but encourage others with a love encounter. Scripture says, those who love me keeps my commands, not those who fear me. Christianity culture has such a religious, and traditional aspect that has taken people from one prison and placed them in another. God is sovereign, and because we are made in His image we are sovereign as well. God wants willing individuals to be a part of the kingdom, not robots. Robots have no mind of their own, and have no heart at all. We cannot force the world to live according to a set of standards that they don't understand. In love, we need to introduce them to Christ, and allow Him to change their inner being from one full of sin, to one that learns and loves to worship God. It is a process, and we must be gentle with those who are lost, and those who are being molded. It's not easy, and the process have the tendency to create very sensitive, and emotional individuals. We come to Christ already broken, our everyday lives, and perspectives are being challenged. God is intentional, and very strategic at the breaking process. He knows the right place, and time to allow the enemy to attack, and how much pressure we can handle without being destroyed. God then steps in, loving us back to life, crushing the enemy under our feet. We need to be like God, in the fact that we love people back to life. This may seem difficult, but it is our responsibility as heirs to the kingdom, and co-laborer with God. Let's step away from rioting, and protesting, try loving someone who is broken. Genuine love will change one life at a time, and eventually the world. Rioting is destructive, and causes chaos. Protesting has only gotten us so far. God holds the ultimate, and final key to locking up hell. So, let's get out of the way, and let God have total control, so we can be true examples of 2 Chronicles 7:14!

READY AIM FIRE...

Love: The Effective Weapon

Session 1: Love is Patient 5

Session 2: Love is Kind 9

Session 3: Love does Not Envy 15

Session 4: Love does Not Boast 19

Session 5: Love is Not Proud 23

Session 6: Love does Not Dishonor 28

Session 7: Love is Not Selfish 33

Session 8: Love is Not Quick to Anger 38

Session 9: Love keeps No Record of Wrong 43

Session 10: Love does Not Delight in Evil, but Rejoices with the Truth 49

Session 11: Love Always Protects 55

Session 12: Love Always Hopes 61

Session 13: Love Always Perseveres 67

Session 14: Love Never Fails 72

Help! Lifestyle of a Worshipper

Session 1: Worship 102

Session 2: In the Name of Jesus 111

Session 3: The Battle Preparation Plan 120

Session 4: Temptation 129

Session 5: Eye for an Eye **138**
Session 6: Jesus vs. The Pharisees **147**
Session 7: What's Your Ending **156**

Hello: Fasting on the Other Side

Session 1: Fasting **167**
Session 2: 3 Day Fast **172**
Session 3: 10 Day Fast **176**
Session 4: 21 Day Fast **180**

Author's Bio

Denise Flippen is a fun, bold, and fearlessly loving Woman of Faith. That is how I would describe myself… I grew up in the city of Lackawanna, and Buffalo, NY. I've always had big dreams to be successful in the medical field. I wanted to be a doctor as a little girl, but those dreams changed as I grew older. Due to my great ability, and desire to debate, I began to consider a career in law. My life took a course of its own, decreasing the value that I had in my ability to achieve such high goals. The lack of love and affection growing up, sent me on a search looking for love in all the wrong places. I had my first child at 15 years of age, and was told that I would be nothing more than a welfare recipient. My view of church was hell and fury. An angry God full of wrath. The love God had for me was limited to John 3:16, and a song, "Yes, Jesus loves me, for the bible tells me so." Where was this love? I never felt much love from God, or those who claimed to know Him, my mother included. My exposure to Christianity was limited to, "You can't do this! You can't do that! Your gonna bust hell wide open!" These are false representations of the loving God we serve. Not saying that there aren't boundaries, but a relationship with God isn't limited to following a set of rules. Four children later, a 13-year relationship, and working as a medically fragile child nurse, I found myself with a bottle of pills in my mouth. I wanted to swallow so badly. I was miserable, and didn't know how to handle it. I never found the love I was so desiring. Not in my children, not in my boyfriend, and not in the money I was making either. I was done! Then God spoke, "Good… right where I need you! You're done?" He questioned. I was complete done. Over this life. "Then you will let me live this life through you." He continued. I went through a couple of weeks struggling, but I knew I was surrendering my life to God. He began giving me instructions, and showing me who He was. I like to call it the, "wooing stage". The first thing God had me to do was to let my relationship go. He didn't say it was sin. He informed me that there was work to be done with him, and if I wanted change, I had to let go. As hard as it was, I walked away. He instructed me to give up the house, job and cars. I walked away from it all. I was left with nothing, but 4 children to carry along on this journey, and God. Truth be told, God is all you need on this journey. My beautiful sister Ebony was also with me, she was going through a journey of her own. I won't share much of her journey, but I will say, God told her to let her 2 jobs go as well, and she obeyed. We were broke!!! And pretty much homeless!!! We received shelter from a worldly cousin who allowed us to stay in her home for free. I express the fact that she's not in Christ to show contrast between those I encountered who claimed to represent Christ, and those who didn't. Thanks, Shavon Petty. She never asked for a dime. My aunt, a Christian woman who owned the home, wanted to increase the rent once my cousin moved out, from $500 monthly to $550 monthly, because I had more children. Never giving us a chance to show what God will do, she looked at our income, and said we had to move as well. Nowhere to go, God made a way for us. (Just a side note, to this day no one has moved into the apartment.) We moved into a hotel, and lived there for 3 ½ weeks. Our bill was $629 weekly. That was an amazing experience watching God provide. Still, so many times, I wanted to remove myself from this journey, and just go back to work. I had visions of me hitting the Powerball, so strong that I told people that I would. Everyone thought I was crazy and laughed at me, especially my mother. She constantly called me delusional during this journey. Everyone would simply suggest that I go back to work. But, I couldn't! There was a pull I couldn't resist. God said, "Nothing your hands could do!" He wanted me to know Him. Know Him as the GREAT I AM! Everything I need, He is!!! After leaving the hotel, we reluctantly went to my mother's house. Boy oh Boy… this was a difficult, and humbling arrangement. This was in April, and it was still snowing some days, and very cold outside. This lasted approximately one month. My mother's husband threw me, my sister and my kids out one night as he was roaming like a roaring lion seeking whom to devour. I was trying to be the peace maker between him, and my sister as he was raging. I was called into the situation and ultimately became the object of his fury. But, I held on to truth, and truth says that nothing can happen to me that God doesn't allow, and if He allows it, it's purpose to it! My best friend gave me and my children shelter for the night. Funny thing, she was another worldly friend, but glory to God her being by my side this entire journey has opened her eyes to truth, and she has discovered God for herself! How could such an ugly journey cause someone to fall to their knees to seek such a God?

May 8th, I consider the date I entered my wilderness journey. I moved into the house my grandmother had left to me years prior. I now call it my ark. The house needed tons of work, and I had no money. My aunt who had previously put me out, did offer money to help, but God told me no! So, I moved into this 2-bedroom upper with no lights, no gas, and no water. God always made a way for us. It took 2 weeks to get electricity turned on. They refused to turn the gas on due to a large gas leak that I couldn't afford to get fixed. The water was on, but there were leaks in the basement stopping water flow to the upper apartment. There were so many people helping me during this time, it is truly too many to name. Just know that God sent me true blessings, and I am truly appreciative for you all. Our house was full of buckets of water to complete daily task. Showers had to be taken at friends and family houses. Thanks Nichole Crouch and Yakenna and Maurice Burse. But, there was one person who never even called to see how we were doing… my mother. I highlight my mom, because this is the one we expect to get the most help and love from. My mother isn't a drug addict or even one who is lost in the streets. She has a Prophet title, and profess to be, "save, sanctified, and Holy Ghost filled. She attends church regularly, and serves. This is in no way to bring **about shame on my mother, but to show how Christianity has been watered down,** missing the true AGAPE (LOVE) factor. I must mention my aunt Jackee Stokes, who was there beyond what I can even imagine. She called, came by, and loved me during this difficult time. **John 14:18** says, *"I will not leave you as orphans; I will come to you."* Jesus was speaking of His Spirit returning after departed earth and returned to His Father. This scripture spoke volumes in my life as I was reminded that God will never leave me alone. And, not only the Holy Spirit that lives in me, but His Spirit which dwells in His people, to be what we need at that moment. I am so appreciative for such a promise.

I had a pride issue and didn't want people knowing what was going on in my life. It was embarrassing, But God promises to give us a double portion for our shame. **(Isaiah 61:7)** I had a friend who attended the same church, Marissa and her husband Paul who wanted to help, but needed more assistance. My sister encouraged me to share my story with my church. I had a meeting our administrator, and the meeting seemed promising. For months, nothing… I had given up. The meeting was in September, it was now December. It was getting extremely cold outside. My children, and I was limited to a bedroom with an electric heater, still gathering buckets of water; however, this time not from neighbors, but now from the basement. We were so thankful to be able to gather water from the basement! The only thing that as keeping me grounded and moving forward was the hope that God placed in my heart. God continuing to assure me that all of this had a purpose kept me persevering. My friend Marissa and Paul wanted to help desperately. My sister, who was on her own journey, and no longer living with me, began doing small catering jobs. She happened to complete one job, and gave me her profit to get the necessary supplies to fix my water and gas lines. Marissa, and her husband Paul came through for me.

Matthew's Heating and Cooling took the job free of charge. I'm so thankful for them! This all took place the first week of December. God held the weather back with His mighty hands. He ensured that I knew He was working on my behalf. All the work was completed on a Saturday. I called the gas company, and they came out that same day. But, the furnace was shot. The electric heater mysteriously stopped working the night before, and the house was freezing. I sent my kids to my mother's house for the night. I had a horrible, "ready to give this whole God thing up experience." I was broken, and finally over it all. I was going back to work and taking my life in my own hands. My friend Marissa is the bomb! She never really cared about my physical needs as much as she did my spiritual. She knew I was breaking down, and she encouraged my spirit, not my flesh, while at the same time, brainstorming ways in which they could assist in meeting some of my physical needs as well. They didn't just talk, they put action behind their love. She showed up at my home with her husband. He checked the furnace, while she took me back to her home to enjoy an evening fun of food, and laughter. My spirit was completely lifted. This is an example of a devoted friend in Christ. It wasn't convenient, but she deemed it important. When Paul returned with the sad news that my furnace was too much to repair, I didn't freak. My hope was restored. The enemy was working overtime to break me, because my break through was present. Satan's tactics are no match for the God that we serve. You may take a hit, but don't you stay down. True friends coupled with the love of Christ helps us back up. The very next day while on my way to church, I bumped into a woman, Roberta whom I had previously prayed with. We had exchanged pieces of our

Author's Bio

storm, and were encouraging each other. She asked for my number because she had a friend who was plumber, and wanted to help me. I informed her that the lines had been fixed, and I needed a new furnace. The very next day, while I was in class, I received a call from a guy who was Roberta's friend. He said he wanted to help, and would be at my home that evening. I warned him that I had no money, and didn't know how I would be able to assist at all financially. He wasn't looking for money, he simply wanted to help. That evening he came out as promised, and checked the furnace. He returned the following day, bring along with him the necessary tool and supplies to fix the furnace. We had heat! Glory to God! God told me nothing that my hands could do. It snowed the next day!

During that journey, I saw the true face of many people. Those who represent Christ, and the world. God could have spoken change into my life just as He spoke the world into existence. How would that have helped me. Leaving me in the fire, and walking it out with me has changed my heart. My heart has been forever changed! I refuse to be one who represent Christ in words or name only. I can't help but to live a life that worships and reflects the love of God. How dare we allow the world to put our love to shame. This is a short, condensed version of course, but there were many, many more things that took place, and many, many more people who were involve. If I didn't mention your name, don't fret, God knows who you are, what you did, and you will reap accordingly.

I do however have to give a special shout out to One Church LA. I feel as if I belong to your church. I tune in regularly, and moved every time. Sarah Roberts, has helped me beginning with a sermon titled, "Empty Hands" You let me know that I wasn't delusional, and that God did have a purpose for my life. You spoke everything God had said to me as if you were there. Your spirit helped me to push forward, and not look back as tough as it was. Touré and Sarah Roberts, spoke into my life consistently, whether it was conformation or instructions. You guys are the real deal! May the Lord continue to bless your ministry! Juanita Bynum, you have also spoke heavily into my life. Not all things you say can I agree with, but it comes from a place of sincerely loving the Lord and wanting people to get it right. You have a passion that I love, a little traditional that can push people away. I was criticized for listening to you. But, when God speaks, God speaks! You didn't push me, you actual drew me closer to you, and a deeper hunger for the Word of God. God, bless you love. My Renovation family, you have been my first encounter with a church who through love, and freedom gave me a desire to seek earnestly after God's love, which truly changes a heart. Your stance on searching self brings about awareness of our own faults in earthly relationships. This reality challenged me to be a better me in spite of those that I am in relationship with. The way you conduct (bible study) community groups are simply amazing, and where I truly discovered God. I recognize the importance of accountability circles.

To everyone who's reading this book. The Holy Spirit is necessary for this journey. Everyone's journey is specific to oneself. God sends servants to help, but everyone won't get how God is calling you to move, or the lack thereof. You must know God for yourself, and trust the Spirit within you. Don't run from people because you don't like what they say. Let the Spirit within you decipher the message. The Holy Spirit is a filter, and will throw away what you don't need, and confirm the things that you do. Conviction is hard, but it is necessary, and needs to become your best friend. It will steer you in the right direction when you are getting off track. You'll need conviction, and confirmation to successfully walk out this journey.

You will read a poem that I wrote later pertaining to how I felt, and the rejection I constantly experienced. The reality is this. My mother only did what she knew to do to protect herself. God has told me, at the end of all of this, I would be the one to love, and care for my mother when she could no longer. And, I am humbly honored to have such a task. In the meantime, I will continue to love my mother. I pray for the breaking of chains in her life. For her to first accept the completely free love that God has for her, so that she may be able to freely love herself, which will eventually flow through her to those around her.

This book is full of lessons that God has taught me, and I am honored to now share them with you. My one desire is to let everyone know that they are loved. This love will help you to Live Out Victories Every Day! Be blessed!

LOVE:
THE EFFECTIVE WEAPON

Introduction

What is Love?

Define love.

_____

_____

According to the Apostle Paul, "Love is patient, love is kind. It does not boast, it's not proud. It does not dishonor others, it is not self-seeking, it is not easily angered, and it keeps no record of wrong doings. Love does not delight in evil, but rejoices with the truth. It always protects, always hopes, always perseveres." **(1 Corinthians 13:4-7)** The Apostle continues in Ephesians praying, "May we be able to comprehend with all the saints what is the width and length and depth and height to know the love of Christ which passes all knowledge." **(Ephesians 3:18)**

The word "love" has been interchanged in the NIV from the word "charity" in the KJV. That is something to think about. Have you ever thought about love as actually being charity? What does charity mean to you?

_____

_____

You don't have to pay anything for God's love. It is freely and voluntarily given to you. God just simply love you and there is nothing that you can do about it. Nothing you can do can separate you from the love of God. **(Romans 8:31-39)** The best thing we could do is to accept God's love, and allow His love to transform our lives.

Do you know how much God loves you? Many sermons are peached about the love of God using, "For God so loved the world, that He gave His only begotten Son, that whoever believes in Him shall not perish but have eternal life." **(John 3:16)** What does that mean to you?

_____

_____

_____

Do hearing this scripture pull at your heart to surrender to a God that is life changing?

_____

_____

_____

When the pastor explains how he has a son, but he's not putting his son to death for the world, and he puts all type of emotion behind it, you feel a transfer of emotions. But, is it enough of a feeling to change your life? _____

In this study, we are going to go deep into detail as to the way that God loves us. We are going to unpack the attributes of the love that the Apostle Paul speaks of. By the end of this study I promise, you will have a better and deeper knowledge of the love that God has for all of us, and how His love changes us, for our love to change others. Our weapon of war is Love, and our ammo is the attributes. By the end of this study we will be load. So, let's get

Ready!!!!

Session 1

Love is Patient

What is patient? Webster defines patient as *"the capacity to accept or tolerate delay, trouble, or suffering without getting upset or angry."* Even when you go see a physician you are considered a patient. You must wait to be seen, wait for a diagnosis, wait for treatment and wait for healing. It's all about waiting. How does waiting make you feel?

_____

_____

_____

If you look closely at the definition of patient, it doesn't give you a time frame. Patience is timeless. Patience and God has something in common. Let's read John 7:1-13 together.

After this, Jesus went around in Galilee. He did not want to go about in Judea because the Jewish leaders there were looking for a way to kill him. But when the Jewish Festival of Tabernacles was near, Jesus' brothers said to Him, "Leave Galilee and go to Judea, so that your disciples there may see the works you do. No one who wants to become a public figure acts in secret. Since you are doing these things, show yourself to the world." For even His own brothers did not believe in Him. Therefore, Jesus told them, *"My time is not yet here; for you any time will do. The world cannot hate you, but it hates me because I testify that its works are evil. You go to the festival. I am not going up to this festival, because my time has not yet fully come."* **After He had said this, He stayed in Galilee. However, ever after His brothers had left for the festival, He went also, not publicly, but in secret. Now at the festival the Jewish leaders were watching for Jesus and asking, "Where is He?" Amongst the crowds there was widespread whispering about Him. Some said, "He is a good man." Others replied, "No, He deceives the people." But no one would say anything publicly about Him for fear of the leaders.**

(John 7:1-13)

There is much that can be discussed from this passage. Take a moment and exchange ideas about your feelings and thought pertaining to this passage. I want to discuss the lack of patience the disciples had verse the patients that Jesus displayed. We all have boundaries in which we are willing to wait. It varies person to person. We are not God who is patient beyond our understanding, but He does require us to grow in loving like Him, which entails growing in patience. In the passage, we just read, the disciples are starting to grow impatient with Jesus lack of public notary. They are growing in their faith of who He is, but still have some doubt. They are looking for validation from the world. They are feeling the need to validate what they are believing by comparing thought with others. But, Jesus knew that the appropriate time had not come. They were not strong enough to hear the option of others. Other people's opinion may have a negative effect on their growth. They still needed time to grow in the confidence of who God is. Their roots need to be planted and needed to be sturdy for where they were headed. Are you looking forward to anything in your life right now that you must practice patience for? How can sharing your exciting news prematurely effect your waiting experience?

_____

_____

See, Jesus knew what was ahead. The Jewish leaders were looking for a way to kill Him. The enemy is looking for a way to kill you, your dream, your hope, and your faith just like they were plotting to kill Jesus. After everyone had left Jesus stayed behind. He was not in the place where His enemies expected Him to be. What if Jesus had given in to the impatience of His brothers? How do you think Jesus being murdered secretly on His way to the festival, before completing all He was set out to do, would have affected the spread of Christianity today?

_____

_____

Let's be more practical. How is your patience when you are trying to make a call and can't get a live representative on the phone? 'Boy' do those automated systems work my nerves. How about language barriers that make it difficult to communicate? Is you patient? Next time you have a language barrier issue, think about how difficult it must be for them to communicate daily. Maybe then you'll have a little more patience. They are coming to a foreign land, leaving everything they really know behind, in hopes of finding a better way of living. Think of how difficult that must be for them. It takes great patience on their behalf to continue to push forward. Your patience with them need be only temporary. But, are you showing patience, or adding difficulty to their already difficult life?

If we can't show patience to a customer service representative, how can we display patience to those who we encounter daily? We are the physical representation of God's love, grace and patience. "Now you are the body of Christ, each one of you is a part of it." **(1 Corinthians 12:27)** How is your patience with your children? Your spouse? Your neighbor? The grocery store attendant? Are they seeing Christ in your life?

For a period of about 40 years He put up with them in the wilderness

(Acts 13:18)

How long has God put up with your disobedience, disrespect, worshiping of idols, and all types of foolery while you were living in the world?

Thank you Father for never giving up on me. I have consistently turned my back on you. But you have been abounding in patience to guide me back to where I belong.

Journal

Over the course of the week look for ways to practice patience personally. Also, look for ways to show patience with others.

Day1: _____
_____
_____
_____

Day2: _____
_____
_____
_____

Day3: _____
_____
_____
_____

Day4: _____
_____
_____
_____

Day5: _____
_____
_____
_____

Day6: _____
_____
_____
_____

SESSION 2

LOVE IS KIND

**Be Kind to one another, tenderhearted, forgiving one another,
even as God in Christ forgave you.
(Ephesians 4:32)**

Being kind speaks to a character that we must possess to represent Christ effectively. Kind is defined as, *"having or showing a friendly, generous, and considerate nature."* We are called to take into consideration other people's feelings. Not quite sympathy. Sympathy is feeling pity or sorrowful. But more like empathy. Empathy is defined as, *"the ability to understand and share the feelings of another."* Try take stepping outside of your comfort zone to see things from a different point of view. We must get to a point where we can look at others' perspective. Everyone grew up differently, so not everyone has the same point of reference. Our perspectives are shaped based upon our upbringing, our surroundings, the era in which we were raised, our access to outward sources (television, internet, magazines, media etc.), and exposure to diverse cultures. What was your upbringing like?

_____

_____

_____

How much exposure did you get to cultures different then your own, including ethnicity and religions?

_____

_____

_____

How has it shaped your opinion, and interactions with people who look, think and believe differently and then you? _____

_____

_____

_____

As Christians God gives us instructions on how we are to handle the challenging task of navigating these types of relationships.

Gently instruct opponents, in hope that God will grant them repentance leading them to a knowledge of truth.

(2 Timothy 2:25)

This is not an invitation to run around and tell people what they are doing is wrong. That helps no one. In fact, that pushes people away. Think of a school age child who has difficulty learning. They try, try and try, but they just can't seem to get it. Typically, this student then becomes the class clown or trouble maker, because of their insecurities connected with their disability. They began to push people away who's trying to help them, out of fear of being exposed. They rather receive consequences than run the risk of being outcast, talked about, made fun of. To protect themselves they harden their hearts and say, "I don't care!" Sometimes the, "I don't care" is verbal, most times it's behavioral, and often, it is both. `

Let's look at a very common barrier using a familiar story. We'll view this story from Pharaoh's perspective, "Pharaoh vs. Moses" or "Pharaoh vs. The Hebrews" and "Pharaoh vs. God", but who thinks about, "Pharaoh vs. His Ancestors"

Let's look at this for a moment. The Hebrews had been living in Egypt for 400 years. The way Pharaoh saw his family treat the Hebrew's was normal to him. He was raised to be god over the Hebrew's and according to his belief, and the responses he received, he was right. The Hebrews lived in captivity so long that they began to take on the practices of the Egyptians. They ate like the Egyptians, partied like the Egyptians and worshipped like the Egyptians. (When in Rome, you do what Romans do.) So, Pharaoh wasn't technically wrong in his behavior. He knew no different. This was simply a way of life for him and his family.

LOVE IS KIND

So, God enters the scene sending a messenger, Moses. He tells Pharaoh that God say, "let his people go". It doesn't surprise me that Pharaoh said, "no". I would say, "Who is this God that you speak of? I don't know this God. It seems to me like you're trying to pull a fast one 'murderer'". Reminding someone usually is all you need to get the pressure off yourself, and your own ugliness. Remember, prior to this Moses had fled from Egypt due to catching a body…lol. He was on the run. Tell me who commits a murder, and then return to the crime scene, and not only return to the crime scene, but approach the very person you were running from? I would suggest if you were going to return you'd have some serious power with you. And Moses did, but Pharaoh didn't know that. See the gods that Pharaoh worshipped was on his side. He did what everyone did before him, and there were no problems. Then Moses appears and you expect him to change up how he's living? That's how the world feels when you approach them telling them to give up something for a God they don't even know. They don't care what comes out of your mouth, you could be telling them anything. They need to experience God, not hear your explanation of Him.

The first time that Moses comes to Pharaoh saying, "God said let my people go." (**Exodus 7:8-8:15**) This started a battle between Moses and Pharaoh, so he thought. As Moses and Aaron perform miraculous signs from the power that God gave them, so did Pharaoh's magicians. This gave Pharaoh less respect for Moses. Although Moses proclaims to be coming in the name of God, Pharaoh was doing the same thing Moses was doing. What are you doing to show people that your God is different from theirs?

_____
_____
_____

How have people who've tried telling you to let your stuff go, while walking around the same behavior as you, had a direct effect on your relationship or lack thereof with

_____
_____
_____

God says, "I'll show him who sent you." And God send Moses and Arron again with the 3rd plague. **(Exodus 8:16-19)** This plague is different. In fact, the magicians could no longer imitate Moses. Pharaoh's magicians began telling him, "this is the finger of God.", but Pharaoh continued to harden his heart.

Then the Lord said to Moses, *"Go to Pharaoh and say unto him, 'this is what the Lord, the God of the Hebrews, says: "Let my people go, so that they may worship me." If you refuse to let them go and continue to hold them back the hand of the Lord will bring a terrible plague on your livestock in the field-on your horses, donkeys and camels and cattle, sheep and goats. But the Lord will make a distinction between the livestock of Israel and Egypt, so that no animal belonging to the Israelites will die.'"* **The Lord set a time and said,** *"Tomorrow the Lord will do this in the land."* **And the next day the Lord did it: All the livestock of the Egyptians died, but not one animal belonging to the Israelites died. Pharaoh investigated and found that not even one of the animals of the Israelites had died. Yet his heart was unyielding and he would not let the people go.**

(Exodus 9:1-7)

plagues began to change. At this point, God, has called for a distinct separation
he Egyptians and the Israelites. God is very strategic when He is calling for change.
stinction that we should have, is between those who represent Christ and the world.
n of life and death is in the way we love. Love is the finger print of God on our
have a finger print or just a simple illusion?
uld have humbled himself and fell under God's grace, but his eyes were fixed
n and the Israelites. He was accustomed to the way things were that he
d who he could be. He had a loyalty to his ancestors and their teachings.
y lye? Is it to man or God? The enemy has a job to do. That's to steal
. He can only do that by causing division. Here he goes trying to
rates with His finger prints of **love**, and the enemy separates with

For our struggle is not against flesh and blood, but against the authorities, against the powers of this world and against the spiritual forces of evil in the heavenly realms.

(Ephesians 6:12)

Thank you Father for searching the inside of us and not our external to call us your children. Thank you for not discriminating against us based upon race, culture or religion.

JOURNAL

This week take an in depth look at self. Record moments that bring you to look, or behave not so kindly toward people who don't look, think, behave, or believe like you. Attempt to go the extra mile to be kind to someone who you deem different.

Day1: _____
_____
_____
_____

Day2: _____
_____
_____
_____

Day3: _____
_____
_____
_____

Day4: _____
_____
_____
_____

Day5: _____
_____
_____
_____

Day6: _____
_____
_____
_____

SESSION 3

LOVE DOES NOT ENVY

Envy is defined, *"a feeling of discontented or resentful longing aroused by someone else's possessions, qualities or luck."* It's also defined as, *"as a desire to have a quality, possession, or other desirable attributes belonging to someone else."* We have all have had, and may currently still battle moments where we desire possessions or characteristics that aren't necessarily our own. **"Thou shall not covet." (Exodus 20:17)** Is not as easy as it sounds.

Envy caused Lucifer fall from heaven taking 1/3 of the angels with him. Envy caused the serpent to deceive Eve, getting her and Adam to disobey God, creating a fallen world. But, we're going to take a quick peek at their sons, Cain and Abel.

Abel kept flocks, and Cain worked the soil. In the course of time Cain brought some of the fruits of the soil as an offering to the Lord. And Abel also brought an offering-fat portions from some of his first born of is flock. The Lord looked with favor on Abel and his offering, but on Cain and his offering he did not look with favor. So, Cain was very angry, and his face was downcast. Then the Lord said to Cain, *"Why are you so angry? Why is your face downcast? If you do what is right, will you not be accepted? But if you do not do what is right, sin is crouching at your door; it desires to have you, but you must over rule it."* **Now Cain said to his brother Abel, "Let's go out to the field." While they were in the field, Cain attacked his brother Abel and killed him.**

(Genesis 4:2-8)

Cain and Abel were two brothers with two different purposes in life, but they had equal potential in God's eyes. Cain offered random sacrifices of fruit as he chose. Abel on the other hand made God a priority by giving to God his first, therefore God looked favorable upon Abel. How have your lack in making God a priority in life caused you to miss God's favor?

Ready Aim Fire

_____

_____

It's ok, you can get your life on track by making God a priority today. Attending this study and applying these truths to your life will start you heading into the right direction. See, this wasn't the first offering that Cain brought to God without making God a priority. The word says, **"In the course of time…"** Meaning that God wasn't quick to dismiss Cain. The reality is that even after Cain became anger God was still willing to draw closer to Cain and get him on the right path. God spoke directly to Cain, asking him some questions. Ask yourself these same questions. Now answer for your anger.

_____

_____

God even warns Cain that the way he's headed is going to lead to destruction. So, God tells him that he should do what he knows it right and that he may have the same favor that his brother has. He then tells him that if he continues choosing anger, sin will snatch him up and take control of him. I think it's safe to assume Cain knew what God was talking about because there was no further conversation. Cain never responded. The word of God tells us that warning comes before destruction. What have God been warning you about that you are playing with?

_____

_____

After the warning, Cain still had the opportunity to get it right, but he allowed his anger to consume him. His anger lead to the infamous killing of his very own brother.

Let's look at two scriptures that speaks to the anger that Cain had in his heart toward his brother.

But I tell you that anyone who is angry with a brother or a sister will be subject to judgement.

(Matthew 5:22)

Anyone who hates his brother or sister is a murderer, and you know that no murderer has eternal life residing in him.

(1John 3:15)

Why do you think that anger and hatred are viewed in the same regards as murder?

_____

_____

We have all been guilty of killing our brother. For one reason or another, we have stored up anger which turned to hatred toward someone. Hatred leads to destructive behavior. It doesn't have to be a physical death, but what about the harsh word we say that can kill confidence, or destroys someone's reputation. This behavior does not only affect the other person's life, but have a major impact on our life as well.

What are some ways that anger, or hatred has caused you to create chaos in someone's life? How has it also shaped your life?

_____

_____

_____

_____

_____

Thank you for all that you have stored in us to accomplish your purpose, giving us abundant favor from you. Thank you for your warnings when we are getting off track and directing us onto the right path simply because you love us. Thank you Lord for creating each and every one of us with uniqueness, diverse personalities, a variety of gifts, and experience to reach the multitude.

Journal

Often, we rage in hatred and anger to dismiss the unpleasant feelings associated with envy. Try acknowledging the actual feeling. Ask God how you can make Him a priority and to remind you of your own gifts, and favor in your life.

Day1: _____

_____

_____

_____

Day2: _____

_____

_____

_____

Day3: _____

_____

_____

_____

Day4: _____

_____

_____

_____

Day5: _____

_____

_____

_____

Day6: _____

_____

_____

_____

Session 4

Love Does Not Boast

To boast, *"is to talk with excessive pride and self-satisfaction about one's achievements, possession, or abilities."* For this lesson, today we are going to focus on a passage from the book of Matthew.

> *"Be careful not to practice your righteousness in front of others to be seen by them. If you do, you will have no reward from your Father in heaven. So, when you give to the needy, do not announce it with trumpets, as the hypocrites do in the synagogues and on the streets, to be honored by others. Truly I tell you, they have their reward in full. But when you give to the needy, do not let your left hand know what your right hand is doing, so that your giving may be in secret. Then your Father, who sees what is done in secret, will reward you."*
>
> *(Matthew 6:1-4)*

We as people often feel the need to be praised for things that we do, and there's nothing wrong with that to an extent. We need to think about the spirit behind our actions. If we run around doing things for the world to praise us, we'll constantly run around trying to please the world, ultimately losing ourselves. The world is never satisfied. In this sermon, Jesus tell us that when we do for other we do receive a reward, but where do you want your reward to come from? The reward that comes from the accolades of the world is pride, we'll talk more about pride next session, but pride comes right before the fall. What are some way that people have praised you, or your accomplishments causing your ego to swell?

_____

_____

The blessing of the Lord brings wealth without painful toil for it.
(Proverbs 10:22)

Without painful toil isn't referring to the laboring we put in to survive. One of the punishment that God gave to man was to sweat from his brow to survive. **(Genesis 3:19)** That's hard work, and God meant what He said. This painful toil is referring to always trying to please man and the pain that comes with never being good enough. How do you feel when you go the extra mile just to go unnoticed?

_____

_____

The Apostle Paul, however does teach us that boasting can be beneficial. Let's look at two scriptures, one from the Apostle Paul and the other written in a letter from John. We'll discuss how the two coincide.

Therefore, I will boast all the more gladly about my weakness,
so that Christ's power may rest on me.
(2Corinthians 12:9)

They triumphed over him by the blood of the Lamb and the word of their testimony.
(Revelation 12:11)

Testimony is defined as, *"evidence or proof provided by the existence or appearance of something."* The proof of the power of God in your life requires bragging about your weakness and inability. When we share with others the power of God in our lives, we give people hope that they too may experience grace and strength. It also boosts to our confidence that, we can do all things through Christ who strengthens us. **(Philippians 4:13)**

Do you understand how boasting about your weakness helps you to triumph over the enemy? Do you encourage others by boasting about your weakness? How does it make you feel?

_____

_____

_____

_____

_____

Remember they deemed Jesus weak when He was upon the cross. Jesus didn't attempt to prove them wrong by coming down, as He could have. He waited for His weakness in the flesh to be transformed to perfect Power, through His death, given by His father. He proved them wrong when He rose again.

Thank you, Jesus, for not feeling the need to prove a point. They humiliated you, called you names, tore your flesh, and hung you to die in a shameful, painful way. You could have called quits and showed your strength for all to see, but you chose to save humanity, and wait for our Father to raise you up. Thank you for dying so that the same strength and power to overcome the enemy now live in me.

Journal

I challenge you to share your weakness with someone in hopes of helping them to overcome a weakness in their own life.

Day1: _____
_____
_____
_____

Day2: _____
_____
_____
_____

Day3: _____
_____
_____
_____

Day4: _____
_____
_____
_____

Day5: _____
_____
_____
_____

Day6: _____
_____
_____
_____

SESSION 5

LOVE IS NOT PROUD

Proud is defined as, *"having or showing a high or excessively high opinion of oneself or one's importance."* Now there is nothing wrong with self-confidence, but there is a difference when it's pride. Pride involves one putting himself on a peddle stool. When we lift our self above others, we tend to then look down on others. In all honesty, at the root of pride is a lack of self-esteem. Pride creates uncomfortable situation for everyone a prideful person encounters.

Pride goes before destruction, a haughty spirit before a fall. It is better to be lowly in spirit along with the oppressed than to share plunder with the proud.
(Proverbs 16:18-19)

A haughty spirit is one that is high, filled up with hot air, the person is full of themselves. What happens when a person becomes full of themselves? What type of behavior can you typically expect from such individuals?

_____
_____
_____

Would you want to share space and wealth with one who is full of themselves? Explain,

_____
_____
_____

Ready Aim Fire

A person full of themselves cannot be full of God, or full of love because they are full of themselves. This leaves no room for God, or others. This easily relates to our discussion last session about boasting. What did we say about boasting?

_____

_____

_____

Pride is really a false sense of security. When someone comes around who appears to be more important, one who's proud tends to feel uneasy, sometimes shying away and other times making a fool of themselves trying to compete for the attention of others, as well as, the one who is currently in the spotlight. This creates an uncomfortable tension for all.

"A certain man was preparing a great banquet and invited many great guests. At the time of the of the banquet he sent his servant to tell those who had been invited, 'Come for everything is now ready.' But they all, alike began to make excuses. The first said, 'I have just bought a field, and I must go see it. Please excuse me.' Another said, 'I have just bought five yoke of oxen, and I'm on my way to try them out. Please excuse me.' Still another said, 'I just got married, so I can't come.' The servant came back and reported this to his master. Then the owner of the house became angry and ordered his servant, 'Go out quickly into the streets and alleys of the town and bring in the poor, the crippled, the blind, and the lame.' 'Sir' the servant said, 'what you ordered has been done, but there is still room' Then the master told his servant, 'Go out to the roads and country lanes and compel them to come in so that my house will be full. I tell you, not one of those who were invited will get a taste of my banquet."
(Luke 14:16-24)

Jesus shared this story to show how God blesses us, but we receive the blessings and turn away in pride. The ones who bought the field, and the five yoke of oxen were too busy for the one who had positioned them in the place to receive such luxuries. I kind of felt bad for the guy who just got married, but that's still no excuse. God blessed this man with his wife.

LOVE IS NOT PROUD

They all have received blessings from the Most High God, and God wanted to honor them more, but they were so consumed with what they had received that they failed recognize that God had more in store for them. What are some blessings that you have received that keeps you too focused to answer the call of God?

_____

_____

_____

The Lord bless and keep you; the Lord makes His face shine upon you and be gracious to you; the Lord turn His face toward you and give you peace.
(Numbers 24-26)

This was a declaration that God gave to His chosen people, the Israelites. You know, the ones that God chose to bless. They became so consumed by the blessing that they left the Blesser hanging. That declaration now belongs to the ones who are willing to come to the table to feast. But don't be like those before you who got so puffed up with hot air that they no longer could sit at the table, being entertained by the temporary gifts God gives. How can you ensure that your blessings will not consume you, making you proud?

_____

_____

I'll give you a tip. Always make time for God. By any means necessary. Stay in communication with Him. When He calls, drop what you need to, to answer. Hold everything loosely. If God gave it once, He can and will do it again.

When someone invites you to a wedding feast, do not take the place of honor, for a person more distinguished than you may have been invited. If, so the host who invited both of you will come and say to you, 'Give this person your seat.' Then, humiliated, you will have to take the least important place. But when you are invited, take the lowest place, so that when your host comes, he will say to you, 'Friend, move up to a better

25

place,' Then you will be honored in the presence of all the other guest. For those who exalt themselves will be humbled, and those who humble themselves will be exalted.
(Luke 14:8-11)

What does this passage mean to you?

_____
_____
_____

How can you practice being humbled?

_____
_____
_____

Remember Jesus washed His disciples' feet... What an amazing example of being humbled.

Thank you Father for sitting high and looking low with love. Thank you for being such an exalted God who thinks so much of mankind that He extends grace to those who are truly beneath Him. You could exist all by yourself, but you chose to in invite nobody's to your table to make us somebody. Thank you, Lord.

Journal

Take this week to think on the many blessings God have entrusted to you, and how you use them. When you feel, pride swelling up, pray and ask God how you can express being humbled. Serving those in need usually helps.

Day1: _____
_____
_____
_____

Day2: _____
_____
_____
_____

Day3: _____
_____
_____
_____

Day4: _____
_____
_____
_____

Day5: _____
_____
_____
_____

Day6: _____
_____
_____
_____

SESSION 6

LOVE DOES NOT DISHONOR

To dishonor is, *"to be in a state of shame or disgrace, or to bring shame or disgrace on."*

Keep on loving one another as brother and sisters. Do not forget to show hospitality to strangers, for by so doing some people have shown hospitality to angels without knowing it. Continue to remember those in prison as if you were together with them in prison, and those who are mistreated as if you yourselves were suffering.
(Hebrews 13:1-3)

We are all God's creation whether we like it or not. It doesn't matter the persons' actions, God loves them. It is in fact, the love of God that changes a person's heart toward God. We never know how our encounter with someone will change their day or even their life, therefore we must treat everyone that cross our path with patience, kindness and respect. Is it difficult for you to show respect for those you deem unworthy of respect? Explain.

_____

_____

It doesn't matter why you believe someone isn't worthy of respect, God deems all of us worthy. Shaming someone brings about condemnation, but relating to someone in there wrong and showing God's changes in your life brings about conviction. God is truly the only one who has the power to condemn, it is our job to simply show grace. Let's look at Jesus example of this.

At dawn, He appeared in the temple courts, where all the people gathered around Him, and He sat down to teach them. The teachers of the law and the Pharisees brought in a woman caught in adultery. They made her stand before the group and

Love Does Not Dishonor

said to Jesus, "Teacher, this woman was caught in the act of adultery. In the law, Moses commanded us to stone such women. Now what do you say?" They were using this question as a trap, in order to have basis for accusing Him. But Jesus bent down and started to write on the ground with His finger. When they kept on questioning Him, He straightened up and said to them, *"Let any one of you who is without sin be the first to cast the first stone at her."* **Again, He stooped down and wrote on the ground. At this those who heard began to go away one at a time, the older ones first, until only Jesus was left, with the woman still standing there. Jesus straightened up and asked her,** *"Woman, where are they? Has no one condemned you?"* **"No one sir," she said.** *"Then neither do I condemn you,"* **Jesus declared.** *"Go now and leave your life of sin,"* **(John 8:2-11)**

This is good stuff right here….and packed with the revelation about who God is, and truth about how we are called to be. LET'S UNPACK!

Now verse 2 describes the location of where Jesus was. It says that, "He appeared again at the temple courts" The temple is referred to in the word as a Holy place. "Courts", we all know what court is, but let's let Webster define it, *"a formal legal meeting in which evidence about crimes, disagreements, etc., is presented to a judge and often a jury so that decisions can be made according to the law."* So, they are all in the right place. The Pharisees were law teachers… Lawyers. They brought a woman before Jesus who committed a crime, which makes Him the Judge and the woman the defendant. There were gatherings of people around Him to hear His teachings as He was seated, they are the jurors of her peers. Can you picture it. Look familiar? "This is a charge that is punishable by death per the law," says the lawyers, and they are seeking death penalty. Put yourself in the defendant shoes for a moment. Would you want leniency from the judge and the jurors?

Jesus bends down to write on the ground with His finger. There is something special about Jesus posture when He begins to write on the ground. It says that He bends down. That sound to me like a position representing humbling Himself. Who would Jesus be humbling Himself to if He is in the highest position in the Holy Courts? Could Jesus have been consulting His Father on this case? Surely looks like it.

And He gave to Moses, when He had made an end of communing with him upon Mount Sinai, two tables of testimony, tablets of stone, written with the finger of God. (Exodus 31:18)

(And with His fingers, He began to write on the ground.) Was Jesus communicating with God as the lawyers were presenting their case? Could it be that God was adding to the commands as a case was being presented before Him? This is amazing!

See God doesn't take from His commands, He simply add to it, because mankind have a way of misinterpreting God's intentions. Jesus in all His divinity still had to humble Himself to His Father in heaven, because at the end of the day while on earth He was still a man and had fleshly pulls just like us. While here in the flesh Jesus was subject to fleshly temptations, it was the power within Him that helped Him to overcome. Take time to reflect on Jesus' statements as it relates to judging.

"Even if I testify on my own behalf, my testimony is valid, for I know where I came from and where I am going. But you have no idea where I come from or where I am going. You judge by human standards; I pass judgement on no one. But if I do judge, my decisions are true, because I am not alone. I stand with the Father, who sent me. In your own Law, it is written that the testimony of two witnesses is true. I am one who testifies for myself; and my other witness is my Father, who sent me."
(John 8:14-18)

The law teachers action would have brought about shame and dishonor upon this woman. This type of behavior does not help to bring about change in someone's life. Jesus first dismisses the crowd before dealing personally with the woman's issues. If we look at the order in which the crowd was disbursed we can also see a parallel with today's society. People are taught how to treat other based on their upbringing. Our elders set the standard and model out how we are to behave. We seem to follow our elders when they are right, and even when they are wrong. We must seek Jesus example of leadership if we are going to live this life productively.

How does shaming someone have a negative effect on their growth?

LOVE DOES NOT DISHONOR

_____

_____

_____

When someone feels shamed, they put a guard up. They began to harden their heart toward people, and God if you are a representation of God, out of fear to be embarrassed again. God doesn't shame us. He deals with our sins in private.

Once the crowd disbursed, older to the younger, Jesus addressed the issue at hand. He showed her that everyone has flaws and are in need of forgiveness, then He acknowledges that her sin was wrong, and finally He tells her go and sin no more.

Jesus is the way, the truth and the life… He just so perfectly models out for us how we are to live this thing called life. It's not easy to treat people how they should be treated, but when we look at Jesus example, we sure have a pretty good example of what it looks like to effectively love people.

If you love those who love you, what credit is that to you? Even sinners love those who love them. And if you do good to those who are good to you, what credit is that to you? Even the sinners do that. And if you lend to those from whom you expect repayment, what credit is that to you? Even sinners lend to sinners, expecting to be repaid in full. But love your enemies, do good to them, and lend to them without expecting to get anything back. Then your reward will be great, and you will be children of the Most High, because He is kind to the ungrateful and the wicked. Be merciful, just as your Father is merciful.

(Luke 6:32-36)

Thank you Father for being the Judge and the jury of my peers. Thank you for loving us too much to humiliate us, but also loving us so much that you refuse to allow us to leave unchanged. You extend us love far beyond what we deserve, and far beyond what we could repay. Thank you for showing us mercy when we deserve death.

Journal

How can you honor someone who you feel don't deserve it this week? Maybe someone is incarcerated for action of their own. God still loves them! Maybe it's someone who wronged you… Reach out and extend mercy and grace.

Day1:_____
_____
_____
_____

Day2:_____
_____
_____
_____

Day3:_____
_____
_____
_____

Day4:_____
_____
_____
_____

Day5:_____
_____
_____
_____

Day6:_____
_____
_____
_____

SESSION 7

LOVE IS NOT SELFISH

Selfish is defined as, *"lacking consideration for others; concerned chiefly with one's own personal profit or pleasure."* This week we are going to take an intimate look into the family of a man that God referred to as, *"A man after my own heart."* **(Acts 13:22 & 1 Samuel 13:14)**

After the course of time, Amnon son of David fell in love with Tamar, the beautiful sister of Absalom son of David. Amnon became so obsessed with his sister Tamar that he made himself ill. She was a virgin, and it seemed impossible for him to do anything to her. Now Amnon had an adviser named Jonadab son of Shimeah, David's brother. Jonadab was a very shrewd man. He asked Amnon, "Why do you, the king's son, look so haggard morning after morning? Won't you tell me?" Amnon said to him, "I'm in love with Tamar, my brother Absalom's sister." "Go to bed and pretend to be ill," Jonadab said. "When your father comes to see you, say to him, 'I would like my sister Tamar to come and give me something to eat. Let her prepare the food in my sight so that I may watch her and then eat it from her hands'" So Amnon laid down and pretended to be ill. When the king came to see him, Amnon said to him, "I would like my sister Tamar to come and make some special bread in my sight, so I may eat it from her hand." David sent word to Tamar at the palace: "Go to the house of your brother Amnon and prepare some food for him." So, Tamar went to the house of her brother Amnon, who was lying down. She took some dough, kneaded it, made bread in his sight and baked it. Then she took the pan and served him the bread, but he refused to eat. "Send everyone out of here." Amnon said. So, everyone left him. Then Amnon said to Tamar, "Bring the food here into my bedroom so I may eat from your hands." And Tamar took the bread she had prepared and brought it into the bedroom. But when she took it to him to eat, he grabbed her and said, "Come to bed with me, my sister."

(2 Samuel 13:1-11)

We are going to complete the story, but I feel the need to stop right here for a moment. Let's take it from the top. There was quite some time that Amnon had been seeing Tamar around, spending time with her, and he began to develop some sort of feelings for her that he associated with being in love. So much so the he became sick, unable to do anything besides think of her. The bible says she was a virgin, which implies she was pure and innocent. Her purity, not the fact that she was his sister made her seem out of his reach, or hard to get. This speaks to the way He viewed himself. How would you say Amnon viewed himself in comparison to Tamar?

_____

_____

_____

I believe it is safe to say that Amnon thought quite lowly of himself in comparison to Tamar. She was a woman who is beautiful and pure, he didn't feel like he had what it takes to make her his lady legitimately.

His cousin, a close cousin in fact, scripture calls him his advisor, come in and have a conversation with him. First, he notices the position of weakness that Amnon is in, then he moves in for the kill. Just like the serpent, gaining Eve's attention in the garden with a question, "Did God really say, 'You must not eat from any tree in the garden.'" **(Genesis 3:1)** Jonadab says, "Why do you, look so haggard morning after morning? Won't you tell me?" How do these two question compare to one another?

_____

_____

The questions asked in both passages were asked not solely for an answer, but to provoke emotion from the answer. This type of questioning opens up dialog, which leads to advice that would direct them down a path of destruction. Take note to how he buttered him up first. He didn't call him by his name, he called him in accordance to a position. Calling him by his position gives a false sense of authority. Sounds like jealousy to me. Very quick lesson. Be careful who you are sharing information about your life with. They may be close, but it doesn't mean they have your best interest at heart. There may just be a serpent down inside.

Love Is Not Selfish

Now let's look at the advice Jonadab gave Amnon. Lay in bed, pretend to be sick, ask for your "sister", and request to eat from her hands. Do you see the set up? The man was already weakened by the sin of lustful desires. Now, you want him to lie, adding fuel to the fire, and put him intimately close to the woman who's his affections are set on.

This is Horrible Advice!!!

Amnon never referred to Tamar as his sister. Actually, the writer goes out of the way to create a distinction in their kinship. Why do you think that is?

_____

_____

_____

Them being related had nothing to do with the relationship between them. It only became evident that they were related when the serpent used Jonadab to entered his two cents. Jonadab was simply encouraging Amnon to use "sister" as a tool to get his way. This is the most horrific act of selfishness… So, as the story continues to unfold David enters the scene. Amnon follows Jonadab's advice as foolish as it sounds, and ask their father for Tamar. King David couldn't see the set up. Why do you think that David was so blinded to his son's behavior and request?

_____

_____

_____

Well I'm not trying to keep you guy all year so I promise to discuss David and his own issues, but for today let's just say that David had issues with lust himself. So much so, that it has created mass destruction in his own life. **(2 Samuel 11)** They had a familiar spirit, and spirits don't cause division between one another. **(Matthew 12:26)** So ultimately David sends his daughter into what will be a lifetime of bondage. Can you think of a time when you have been blinded by poor habits of your own, that you willingly or innocently turned a blind eye?

_____

_____

_____

Before we end today lesson, let's take a quick look at Tamar.

Innocently, Tamar follows her father's instructions. She prepared the dough and prepares her brother's meal before him and their servants. As I was reading the story to prepare for this study. I had a revelation that God wants me to share with you guys. This relates to rape and the way that we as a people view different rape scenario's. When the bible refers to bread, it typically represents the body of Christ. Well this time, I envisioned the body of Tamar, and I'm sure Amnon did too. The more she did, as innocent as it may have felt to her, the more enticed he became. To the point that he refused to eat, and ordered everyone around them away. His passion had been taken to the ultimate level and there was no way he could control himself any longer. He didn't care about the consequences. Selfishness (sin) had completely take over him. He calls her to come closer and she obeyed. Why is she not alarmed by his actions? The bible doesn't say that she's drawn to him as well, but she attempts to give him what he's asking for, and then things change. A turn for the worst.

Lets' be careful not to judge others and their situations. We don't have clear insight as to how they ended up in the situations they are currently in. The enemy is very sneaky, and wisely deceptive. We don't know the whole story behind people's actions, but God does. Let God do the judging, and you do the loving.

Thank you Father that you see the whole story. You created the beginning from the end and have set up your grace and mercy for everything in between. You, so selflessly sent your Son to carry the burden of the world, so that our sins may be not only forgiven, but so that we may have grace to accompany us on a journey of turning away from sin. We cannot walk out this journey alone, as the enemy is very wise and tricky. You said if it had not been for your Holy Spirit that even the elect would be fooled. That you for your Holy Spirit that leads and guides us, alerts and warns us. Thank for the strength to take the exits that you so graciously supply when temptation is heavy. Thank you!

JOURNAL

We'll continue this story next session. Take some time to reflecting on your passions or desires and how they could've, or have lead you on the path of destruction. Encourage someone from a place of empathy that you see struggling.

Day1: _____
_____
_____
_____

Day2: _____
_____
_____
_____

Day3: _____
_____
_____
_____

Day4: _____
_____
_____
_____

Day5: _____
_____
_____
_____

Day6: _____
_____
_____
_____

Session 8

Love is Not Quick to Anger

Picking up where we left off last week, I want to encourage everyone to recap very briefly, because we are diving right in.

"No, my brother!" she said to him. "Don't force me! Such a thing should not be done in Israel! Don't do this wicked thing. What about me? Where could I get rid of my disgrace? And what about you? You would be like one of the wicked fools in Israel. Please speak to the king; he will not keep me from being married to you." But he refused to listen to her, and since he was stronger than she, he raped her. Then Amnon hated her with intense hatred. In fact, he hated her more than he had loved her. Amnon said to her' "Get up and get out." "No!" she said to him. "Sending me away would be a greater wrong than what you have already done to me." But he refused to listen to her. He called his servant and said, "Get this woman out of my sight and bolt the door after her." So, his servant put her out and bolted the door after her. She was wearing an ornate robe, for this was the kind of garment the virgin daughters of the king wore. Tamar put ashes on her head and tore the ornate robe she was wearing. Her brother Absalom said to her, "Has that Amnon, your brother, been with you? Be quiet for now, my sister; he is your brother. Don't take this thing to heart." And Tamar lived in her brother Absalom's house, a desolate woman. When king David heard all of this, he was furious. And Absalom never said a word to Amnon, either good or bad; he hated Amnon because he had disgraced his sister Tamar.
(Samuel 13:12-22)

Tamar said, "No!" Not only did she say no, she tried to reason with him. She tried to use the same tactics that he used to get her there in the first place, she called him "brother." She gave him reasons that it was wrong, she pleaded for herself, then she pleaded for him and his

LOVE IS NOT QUICK TO ANGER

reputation. Did Tamar make a good argument? Why do you think that with all the pleading that she was doing, Amnon continued?

_____

_____

_____

Tamar told Amnon to speak to the king and seemed pretty confident that he would allow them to wed. Do you agree that their kinship was just a gimmick Amnon was using to get Tamar alone with him? If not explain.

_____

_____

Tamar seemed to care a great deal for Amnon, she was willing to wed him with the permission from their king. But she was a pure woman, and remaining pure was clearly important to her. She wanted to do things the right way. Amnon was so overcome by sin that he made a decision that would change the both of their lives forever. Sadly, he raped her.

Immediately after he satisfied his lust, he hated her. The scripture say, "He hated her more than he had loved her." Could he have ever truly loved her at all? Love isn't about feelings and emotions; it's about the choosing to love even when we don't feel like loving. Amnon didn't love Tamar, he was simply wrapped up in emotions of lust, which he deemed as love. How have an emotion that you associated with love caused chaos, or driven you to make irrational decisions in your life?

_____

_____

_____

Do nothing out of selfish ambition or vain conceit. Rather, in humility value others above yourselves, not looking to your own interest but each of you to the interests of the others.

(Philippians 2:3-4)

Ready Aim Fire

The fact that Amnon was angry immediately speaks to his lack of love for Tamar, but his actions afterwards were even more alarming. He threw her out as if she was worthless. He did not care about the shame that would be brought upon her. Why do you think he felt such an urgency to get Tamar out and away from him?

_____

_____

Having Tamar in his presence would be a reminder to him of his sin. Have you ever done something so out of character that you wanted every remanence of it erased, even from your mind?

_____

I can relate!

Tamar was so concerned about her reputation that she was still willing, after being violently abused, to cover over the sin, and coexist with her abuser. Often, we find ourselves remaining in secret situations out of fear of what people will say, or think. You don't have to share with the group, but write down a situation that you are being held captive to. Why do you feel stuck? God knows, and he's willing to deliver you. Are you ready?

_____

_____

Tamar immediately began taking on the identity that she feared would be her future. No one had even known, yet Tamar called herself, "shame" She tore her own gown because she deemed herself unworthy, no one had to do it for her. She covered herself with ashes and walked independently into her self- appointed isolation. Have you played judge and jury over you own situation? Have you thrown yourself into a prison, and threw away the keys?

_____

_____

Love Is Not Quick To Anger

The Spirit of the Sovereign Lord is upon me, because the Lord has anointed me to proclaim good news to the poor. He has sent me to bind up the brokenhearted, to proclaim freedom for the captives and release from darkness for the prisoners, to proclaim the year of the Lord's favor and the day of vengeance of our God, to comfort all who mourn, and provide for those who grieve in Zion- to bestow on them a crown of beauty instead of ashes, the oil of joy instead of mourning, and a garment of praise instead of a spirit of despair. They will be called oaks of righteousness, a planting of the Lord for the display of his splendor.
(Isaiah 61:1-3)

Getting upset is not a sin, but we should look at why we are angry to see if our anger is pointed in the right direction. Often times… it isn't! Amnon became angry with Tamar, when if he would have paused to reflect, he would've realized that he should have been angry with himself. And, if he would've paused a little longer, he would've seen the real enemy behind the scenes. The bible tells us that we don't wrestle against flesh and blood, but against evil spirits. **(Ephesians 6:12)** There is a very real enemy who is waiting for you to point the finger at others to keep you in bondage. Even stopping at pointing the finger at yourself, stops you from achieving all that God has for you. Anger will do the trick.

"In your angry do not sin": Do not let the sun go down while you are still angry, and do not give the devil a foothold.
(Ephesians 4:26)

Anger will cause you to do things that you will soon regret. Your sun can set at any time, and you will leave this earth with anger in your heart. Anger have the tendency to elevate blood pressure leading to a stroke or heart attack. Is it really worth it? Here's some advice, once you feel anger stirring up, talk to God about it. Identify where it's coming from, and point your finger in the appropriate direction. Ask God for clarity and precise instructions on how to handle it, then act. You don't want to give the devil a foothold because he will not let go, not without a fight anyways.

Thank you, Lord for your love and kindness. For your grace and compassion, being slow to anger when I often provoke you to wrath, but instead showing me mercy rich in love.

Journal

Being in control of our emotion is not easy to do, but what you do with your emotions is another thing. Don't allow your emotions to supersede your intelligence? Identify the real emotion behind anger, and handle it appropriately.

Day1: _____
_____
_____
_____

Day2: _____
_____
_____
_____

Day3: _____
_____
_____
_____

Day4: _____
_____
_____
_____

Day5: _____
_____
_____
_____

Day6: _____
_____
_____
_____

Session 9

Love Keeps No Record of Wrong Doing

So, this attribute isn't a word that Webster can define, but I'm sure we have all been guilty of keeping a record of wrong doing. You know that little piggy bank full of arsenal to justify any ungodly behavior we display toward a specific person. Today we will be discussing adultery, and although the passage speaks on a woman, take note that this applies to men as well. Simply allow God to minister to you directly. Another quick note: Sometimes we put ourselves in situations that God did not deem. Be very prayful as to how God wants you to move pertaining to your individual circumstance. Don't' allow the opinions of others to override what God is speaking directly to you.

My son, pay attention to my wisdom, turn your ears to my words of insight, that you may maintain discretion and your lips may preserve knowledge. For the lips of an adulterous woman drip honey, and her speech is smoother than oil; but in the end, she is bitter as gall, sharp as a double- edge sword. Her feet go down to death; her steps lead straight to the grave. She gives no thought to the way of life; her paths wander aimlessly, but she does not know it. Now then my sons, listen to me; do not turn aside from what I say. Keep to a path far from her, do not go near her house, lest you lose your honor to others and dignity to one who is cruel, lest strangers feast on your wealth and toil enrich the house of another. At the end of your life you will groan, when your flesh and body are spent. You will say, "How I hated discipline! How my heart spurned correction! I would not obey my teachers or turn my ear to my instructors. And soon in serious trouble in the assembly of God's people." Drink water from your own cistern, running water from your own well. Should your springs run overflow in the streets, your streams of water in the public square? Let them be yours alone, never to be shared by strangers. May your fountain be blessed, and may you

rejoice in your youth. A loving doe, a graceful deer- may her breast satisfy you always, may you ever be intoxicated with her love. Why my son, be intoxicated with another man's wife? Why embrace the bosom of a wayward woman? For your ways are in full view of the Lord and He examines all your paths. The deeds of the wicked ensnare them; the cord of their sins hold them fast. For lack of discipline they will die, led astray by their own great folly.
(Proverbs 5:1-25)

It's funny, because in the natural sense I'm not married, but I am married to Christ and that is just as equally important, actually more. Have you guys ever thought of your relationship with God as a marriage? Explain.

_____
_____
_____

"Do not be afraid; you will not be put to shame. Do not fear disgrace; you will not be humiliated. You will forget the shame of your youth and remember no more the reproach of your widowhood. For the Lord your Maker is your husband- the Lord Almighty is His name- the Holy One of Israel is your Redeemer; He is called the God of all the earth. The Lord will call you back as if you were a wife deserted and distressed in spirit – a wife who married young, only to be rejected," says your God. "For a brief moment, I abandoned you, but with deep compassion I will bring you back. In a surge of anger, I hid my face from you for a moment, but with everlasting kindness I will have compassion on you," says the Lord your Redeemer.
(Isaiah 54:4-8)

What are some ways that you have committed adultery against the Lord?

_____
_____
_____

Love Keeps No Record Of Wrong Doing

How do you feel knowing that He's willing to forgive you?

_____
_____
_____

This by no means am I deeming adultery to be ok. Reading the passage from Proverbs, the adulterous woman seems to be very attractive and conniving. In the passage the woman lips are described as dripping honey. Describe honey's substance and compare it to an attractive woman's lips.

_____
_____
_____

Her speech is described as oil, what is the writer implying?

_____
_____
_____

She is rooted in death, which causes her to be bitter internally. This is describing a woman who has been brought up in pain. She isn't intentionally deceptive, but it's a normal way of living for her. There are insecurities that dictates her every move. She's looking for love, but isn't sure what it looks like, or where to find it. So, she settles for temporary fleshy pleasures that imitate it. She feels she has nothing to lose. Have you ever felt this way in life? If so, what were some of life's issues that caused you to feel this way?

_____
_____

Do you know a woman that we are describing? What can you do to show her a better way of life?

Ready Aim Fire

_____

_____

_____

Typically, we'll see the behavior and judge the persons' actions, not realizing that there are deeper roots. We are called to come alone side the brokenhearted and show them the love of Christ, not to judge and talk about them, causing them more shame. If this woman has effected your life, it's normal to get angry, but don't stay angry. Anger grows roots, that lead to bitterness as we discovered last session. Do you think Tamar could have turned into an adulterous woman? Explain.

_____

_____

_____

We know that trouble is easy to get into, but hard to get out of, so let's look at some ways to avoid the trouble all together. Proverbs tells us to stay away from her house. It doesn't literally mean her house. Our temporary body is often referred to as a house in scripture. If you know that you are attracted to this woman, why take the risk of being involved, or in close proximity. Is it wise? These type of feelings is nothing to be ashamed of, but the enemy wants you to feel shamed, so that you will keep it a secret. Secrets fester, creating an infection inside. The longer you keep it in, the worst it gets, and the deeper it grows. Before you know it, you'll be like Amnon feeling ill and the wrong one will see it. Although it's important to talk to someone, choosing wisely is essential. You don't want someone who will feed your fleshly desirers, but someone who will tell you truth, and hold you accountable. Spiritually wise friends are hard to find. My suggestion is to take it to God in all honesty, holding nothing back letting Him be your sounding board. Ask God to send someone in your life that will help you with your journey. Do you believe you have any spiritually wise friends? Do you trust sharing with them shameful situations? Ask God to reveal to you the true nature of these relationships. If you are married, as difficult as it may seem, have these conversations with your spouse. Honest and open communication is essential in creating and maintaining a healthy marriage.

LOVE KEEPS NO RECORD OF WRONG DOING

Married couples, enjoy one another company. Sex is beautiful and is meant to be enjoyed, but it isn't the only reason people cheat. Spend time with one another, laugh, dance and complement one another. It's easy to get caught up in the likes of the world. Make God the center of your relationship and get caught up in Him together. If your loyalty is to God, then you have nothing to worry about when it comes to loyalty to each other. In the face of temptation, God always provides an escape. **(1 Corinthians 10:13) Take it and run home to your spouse!!!!!** Remember extending grace isn't throwing in each other's face your short comings, but forgetting those things that are former and push toward the mark of the high calling. **(Philippians 3:14)**

Thank you, Father for never giving up on me. You love me despite my flaws.

JOURNAL

Reflect on ways you have turned your back on God, but through His mercy and grace, how He's forgiven you, never to be use against you. Share this reality with someone that feel they have nothing to lose.

Day1: _____
_____
_____
_____

Day2: _____
_____
_____
_____

Day3: _____
_____
_____
_____

Day4: _____
_____
_____
_____

Day5: _____
_____
_____
_____

Day6: _____
_____
_____
_____

Session 10

Love Does Not Delight in Evil, But Rejoices with The Truth

Love does not delight in evil refers to, laughing at someone's pain, secretly or publicly wishing they fail. You know…. Waiting for the, "I told you so," moment. Instead of waiting in hopes of a negative outcome, we are supposed to be rejoicing in the truth. Jesus said, *"I am the way, the **truth**, and the light."* **(John 14:6)** So, what is Jesus' truth?

_____

_____

_____

_____

> **And we know that in all things God work for the good of those who love Him, who have been called according to His purpose. For those God foreknew He also predestined to be conformed to the image of His Son, that He might be the firstborn among many brothers and sisters. And those He predestined, He also called; those He called, He also justified; those He justified, He also glorified. What shall we say to these things? If God is for us, who can be against us? He who did not spare His Own Son, but gave Him up for us all-how will He not also, along with Him, graciously give us all things? Who will bring any charges against those whom God has chosen? It is God who justifies. Who then is the one who condemns? No one. Christ Jesus died-more than that, who was raised to life-is at the right hand of God and is also interceding for us. Who shall separate us from the love of Christ? Shall trouble or hardship or persecution or famine or nakedness or danger or sword? As it is written: "For your sake, we face death all day long; we are considered as sheep to be slaughtered."**

No, in all these things we are more than conquerors through Him who loves us. For I am convinced that neither death nor life, neither angels nor demons, neither present nor the future, nor any power, neither height nor depth, nor anything else in all creation, will be able to separate us from the love of God that is in Jesus our Lord. (Romans 8:28-39)

Now, this is some truth for you. Do you believe these truths? The problem today is that we hear the word, but either don't understand the word or don't believe the word, making it difficult to walk according to the word. How would your life change if you truly believed that your past, present and future circumstances, and actions will not and cannot change the way God loves you?

_____

_____

_____

God is Love! He is the same today, yesterday, and forevermore. **(Hebrew 13:8)** God's love for us isn't the problem, but our willingness to accept is. What makes it difficult for you to accept God's love?

_____

_____

Once you realize that God has a purpose for you, and that your life, your past experiences, hurts and mistakes qualifies you for the task, you will be able to walk in freedom with no shame. Who can condemn you, who can judge you? "No one!" say the Lord. And when people try to prosecute you, remember Jesus is the Judge and the Jury. He will challenge them to cast their stone. Let's take a second look at the story from session 6. Read it if you must. I don't want anyone to think by any means necessary that this passage is a license to sin. It is not! But, if you remember, after all the woman's accusers had left, Jesus spoke to the woman directly. He confirmed what she had done was wrong by telling her, *"go and sin no more."* We must allow God the space and opportunity to discipline and to restore.

Love Does Not Delight In Evil, But Rejoices With The Truth

What, after all, is Apollos? And what is Paul? Only servants, through whom you came to believe-as the Lord has assigned to each his task. I planted the seed, Apollos watered it, but God has been making it grow. So, neither the one who plants, nor the one who waters are anything, but only God, who makes thing grow. The one who plants and the one who waters have one purpose and they will be rewarded according to their own labor. For we are co-workers in God's service; you are God's field, God's building.
(1 Corinthians 3:5-9)

Pretty cool truth, but how do we plant and what do we plant?

_____

_____

Well I'm glad you asked. We plant love with love. Everything we have been leaning is, planting and watering. Once you plant the seed you don't give up on the seed, you continue loving the seed. Trusting that if for some reason, you are disconnected from the seed, that God will send someone to continue to water it. We must share the truth about the love of God with everyone, everywhere. That's how we create true change. And not by talking about it only, but by being an example of it. God is much better experienced than explained. You may be the first encounter someone has with Christ, are you representing Him well? Explain.

_____

_____

_____

You can very well change a life. What needs to be changed within you, to be more effective in planting and watering seeds?

_____

_____

We all can make some changes in the way we love people. God teaches us and changes us daily. Don't resist the change. There are many fields out there ready to be harvested.

Let's speak on one particular field today. We'll call this field, "Trump Field." I want to start by first by acknowledging all the hurtful, demeaning, racist, disrespectful things he has said. The truth is, it doesn't make him less loved by God. He has been placed in a position of power and it was ordained by God, like it not.

Let everyone be subject to the governing authorities, for there is no authority except that which God has established. The authorities that exist have been established by God.
(Romans 13:1)

Not my words, but God's truth. I happen to agree. See the reality is that there is more truth to it. Flip your pages and read the first sentence of the passage from Romans 8:28. Do you believe that truth? If not, please explain and share with your group.

_____

_____

There is purpose for everything that we encounter in life. How can we show empathy to someone if we have never experienced mess? God doesn't just create messy circumstances in our lives, we create them when we make decisions that are contrary to the word of God. We give the enemy a foothold, and then we point our finger at God. God doesn't create the mess, but He is willing to clean it up. Donald Trump, his family and his supporters that follow him for all sorts of reasons, have roots that come from somewhere. We are not in his everyday life, and can't clearly see who God is surrounding him with. We don't know why he make the decisions that he does. But if you believe the **truth**, then I challenge you to believe these two things. You must show love and respect to all people including those who hurt, mistreat and abuse you, because God still loves them. And, trust that all things good, bad and ugly are working for your good, because you love the Lord, and have a purpose to represent Him. It's not easy, but we must be intentional if we are going to bring about change. God doesn't put it on the world to love, He puts it on us…the us who knows Him, who's experienced, and accepted His love. One last passage…

LOVE DOES NOT DELIGHT IN EVIL, BUT REJOICES WITH THE TRUTH

"If my people, who are called by my name, will humble themselves and pray and seek my face and turn from their wicked ways, then I will hear from heaven, and I will forgive their sin and heal their land."

(2 Chronicles 7:14)

God leaves it up to us. If Donald Trump fails, we failed, because the power is in our hands. So, what will you do with your power?

_____
_____

Thank you Lord for not laughing at my mess, but using my mess for your message!

Journal

I know this week was difficult. The bible says, the word cuts like a double edge sword. Let's agree with the truth together, and began to make some fundamental changes. This week pay attention to your emotions and just journal them.

Day1: _____
_____
_____
_____

Day2: _____
_____
_____
_____

Day3: _____
_____
_____
_____

Day4: _____
_____
_____
_____

Day5: _____
_____
_____
_____

Day6: _____
_____
_____
_____

Session 11

Love Always Protects

If you made it this week, I'm glad you're still with me. There has been a lot of convicting and challenging messages so far, and honestly, after last week's message, I wouldn't be surprised if we lost a few people. But, don't be quick to judge. These truths are hard to handle. So, if your buddy isn't here today, give them a call and make sure they are ok. They may need some uplifting this week. Today is going to be equally difficult as we unravel some more truths. Most of the difficulty is due to God calling us to think in a way that we never had to before. Remaining in the study shows strength on your behalf, and a dedication that is required for growth. The journey isn't easy, at first, it's quite hard. But with time, and gaining a revelation of God's perspective of your everyday problems, the load becomes lighter to carry. Enough chatting we have lots to discuss today…

Protect is, *"to keep from harm or injury."* So, we're going back to Romans 13. This time we're going a little deeper and looking a little closer.

Let everyone be subject to the governing authorities, for there is no authority except that which God has established. The authorities that exist have been established by God. Consequently, whoever rebels against the authority is rebelling against what God has instituted, and those who do so will bring judgement on themselves. For rulers hold no terror for those who do right, but for those who do wrong. Do you want to be free from fear of the one in authority? Then do what is right and you will be commended. For the one in authority is God's servant for your good. But if you do wrong, be afraid, for rulers do not bear the sword for no reason. They are God's servants, agents of wrath to bring punishment on the wrongdoer. Therefore, it is necessary to submit to the authorities, not only because of possible punishment but also as a matter of conscience. This is why you pay taxes, for the authorities are God's servants, who give their full time to governing.

Give to everyone what you owe them: If you owe taxes, pay taxes; if you owe revenue, then revenue; if respect, then respect; if honor, then honor.

(Romans 13:1-7)

I'm sure many of you never even seen this in the bible before… This is my first encounter and it has left my mouth wide open. How many of you want to run and check your own bible for reassurance? I understand. This is a tough command to follow considering today's events, and injustices. So, let's break it down concerning today's circumstances.

Much of what I see on Facebook today besides hatred, is fear. I have been pressing in and seeking God about several things in my personal life. One of the most difficult parts of my journey was related to emotions and how I handle them. Before deciding to surrender my life to Christ I had a break down, and with all the power within me I attempted suicide. But there was another power working outside of me that wouldn't allow me to swallow the pills I had in my mouth. I wanted to die. Shortly after that situation, I decided to surrender my life to God. Never to return to the death I was living (sin). Every time hardship would come my way or I would lose hope, I would cry out to God to just end my life. This world seemed too much for me to handle. I believe to be absent from the body is to be present with the Lord. Let's look at what the Apostle Paul take.

For we know that if the earthly tent we live in is destroyed, we have a building from God, an eternal house in heaven, not built by human hands. Meanwhile we groan, longing to be clothed instead with our heavenly dwelling, because when we are clothed, we will not be found naked. For while we are in this tent, we groan and are burdened, because we do not wish to be unclothed but to be clothed instead with our heavenly dwelling, so that what is mortal may be swallowed up by life. Now the one who has fashioned us for this very purpose is God, who has given us the Spirit as a deposit, guaranteeing what is to come. Therefore, we are always confident and know that as long as we are at home in the body we are away from the Lord. For we live by faith, not by sight. We are confident, I say, and would prefer to be away from the body and at home with the Lord. So, we make it our goal to please Him, whether we are at home in the body or away from it. For we must all appear before the judgement seat

of Christ, so that each of us may receive what is due us for the things done while in the body, whether good or bad.
(2 Corinthians 5: 1-10)

When we strive to live a life that is pleasing onto the Lord, one that agrees, and represent respect toward the Lord, we recognize that death isn't such a dreadful thing. We began to look forward to meeting our savior and reaping the rewards He have stored up for us. The problem today is that most people fear death. When our body's experience fear, we have two responses… Fight or Flight! We're taught very early on that a man fights, and a coward take flight, so to save face, many choose to fight. Often, the fight feels like it's a fight for your life.

Think of a situation that forced you to choose between Fight/Flight? What did you choose and why? How did you feel afterward?

_____
_____
_____

We often react in the heat of the moment with self in mind. That's what fear causes you to do. Fear is the counter production of love. Fear cause you to dismiss all the other possible outcomes, and make a choice based off selfish intuition.

Let's define fear. Fear is, *"an unpleasant emotion caused by the belief that someone or something is dangerous, likely to cause pain or a threat."* So, fear is based off perspective. That's a dangerous thing, because as we studied in session 3 our perspectives are incomplete, shaped by our limited upbringings, which creates prejudices. So, we have limited perspectives, coupled with fear, encouraged to fight if we aren't punks, take flight if you're a coward, then give someone a gun and badge and tell them to protect and serve people they don't even know. How do we combat this counter production?

_____
_____

Well, I have the passages that will teach us exactly what we must do and how to do it.

Above all else, guard your heart, for everything you do flows from it.
(Proverbs 4:23)

Do not be anxious about anything, by prayer and petition, with thanksgiving, present your requests to God. And the peace of God, which transcends all understanding, will guard your heart and your minds in Christ Jesus.
(Philippians 4:6-7)

Whoever tries to keep their life will lose it, and whoever loses their life will preserve it.
(Luke 17:33)

Fear and hatred, renders you powerless. Powerless people given power is dangerous. The solution isn't in our protest and anger, but in our love. We must come alongside the broken children of God and love them to Christ. I have a message for those who are broken due to senseless violation of those in position of power. My heart is with you! God sees all, and knows all. We live in a broken, fallen world. We are all flawed people. Let God be your vindicator. Trying to get justice in your own power will only create a bigger mess. Don't allow the actions of another cause you to lose yourself. Use the circumstances to propel you to love harder, and deeper. Your unfortunate circumstances can be used as a catalyst to drive love nationwide, instead of fear, hatred and violence. Be the voice that creates change in the name of peace, love and most importantly, the name of Jesus!

Tremble and do not sin; when you are on your beds, search your hearts and be silent. Offer sacrifices of the righteous and trust the Lord. Many, Lord, are asking, "Who will bring us prosperity?" Let your face shine on us. Fill my heart with joy when their grain and new wine abound. In peace, I will lie down and sleep, for you alone, Lord make me dwell in safety.
(Psalm 4:4-8)

Thank you, Father that all things continue to work for my good even when it doesn't feel that way. Thank you that you are our vindicator and that true justice can only come from you. Thank you for searching the depths of you heart and continuing to love us with a love that brings about change.

Journal

We are coming close to the end of our time together, and have discover so much. The next 3 sessions will bring such about a drastic change in our lives as we look at my testimony. Prepare yourselves by journaling feelings on what we've learned so far.

Day1: _____
_____
_____
_____

Day2: _____
_____
_____
_____

Day3: _____
_____
_____
_____

Day4: _____
_____
_____
_____

Day5: _____
_____
_____
_____

Day6: _____
_____
_____
_____

Session 12

Love Always Hopes

Hope, *"a feeling of expectation and desire for a certain thing to happen."* Our entire lives are full of hope. We expect life to happen as it always does. But, what happens when our hope is met with disappointment. Let's look at a famous passage out of the book of Jeremiah.

"For I know the plans I have for you," **declares the Lord,** *"Plans to prosper you and not to harm you, plans to give you hope and a future. Then you will call on me, and come and pray to me, and I will listen to you. You will seek me and find me when you seek me with all your heart. I will be found by you,"* **declares the Lord,** *"And I will bring you back from captivity. I will gather you from captivity. I will gather you from all the nations and places where I have banished you,"* **declares the Lord,** *"And will bring you back to the place from which I carried you into exile."*
(Jeremiah 29:11-14)

This is one of my favorite passages, but just like many of you, I only knew the beginning, verse 11. Shortly after surrendering my life, my daughter's high school principle gave me this verse. I got instantly excited, "God has plans for me, no harm, hope and a future filled with prosperity." By the way, let's define prosperity, *"a state of being prosperous."* One of the synonyms is successful. What is success to you?

_____
_____
_____

Success is different to many people. Success to me is hearing, "Well done my good and faithful servant." upon entering the heavenly gates. But, there are many rewards on earth that we can gather on this journey called life. Heaven or hell has never been able to motivate me to surrender my life to Christ, it has led me to fear God. Knowing that He loves me, and deems me valuable, that peaked my interest. Ultimately, the icing on the cake was hope for a brighter future. See, nobody tells you the backdrop for the famous Jeremiah 29:11. But I will.

The children of Israel had gotten free from the clutches of Egypt after the plagues that were discussed in session 2. God parted the Red Sea for His children to pass through drowning Pharaoh and his army as they chased them. God provided them manna from heaven to eat and water from a rock as they roamed the wilderness. They received instructions from God himself on a stone table, sealed with the finger print of God. Remember that from session 3? Due to their complaining, fear (after all they seen God do), and ungrateful attitude, God punished them by not allowing the elders to enter the Promised Land. So, they wandered 40 year until the elders died. The next generation entered the land God promised, flowing of milk and honey (prosperity) and defeated enemy after enemy with God on their side. They settled down to enjoy life, and immediately after the death of their leader Joshua, scripture says the next generation began acting a fool. They no longer honored God, but began worshipping things that their hands have made. They lived in pure disrespect, and follow their own fleshly desire. They got proud, full of themselves, remember session 5. Seeing that God is not quick to anger (session 8) God sends messengers to warn them about the destruction they were about to face. Instead of listening and turning from their sin, they try to kill or imprison them. So, God says ok… I've had enough! It's time that I remove my protecting covering off you'll lives, and send you'll into exile. So, when the Israelites received this Jerimiah 29:11 message, they were in captivity and they were sentenced to 70 years. Yeah… I know 70 years' sound like a lot. But we must consider how long did God give them to get their act together. He had to clean up a big mess that they themselves created. God strips them from their blessings, and disciplines them like the loving Father He is. Let's think for a moment parents. When your children are misbehaving do you punish them because you want to create a change, or simply to make them upset with you? God want to create change in our lives as well. Of course, He can snap his fingers, and change our situation in a blink of an eye but, how would that change us? We would end up making the same decisions that landed us in trouble the first time. To help Israel persevere through this tough time God gave them a promise. He began the promise by ensuring them that He isn't trying to harm them.

LOVE ALWAYS HOPES

How does discipline differ from causing harm?

_____

_____

_____

Then He tells them that this won't last forever, giving them hope for a brighter future. He tells them what He expects from them after they're set free from captivity. What does God what in exchange for our free and prosperous life?

_____

_____

_____

Considering all we studied so far, is God's request too much? All He wants is to be first in our lives, so that we don't be overcome by that sneaky devil. Why do you think we make it so difficult?

_____

_____

_____

Do you believe God is causing you harm right now? Well He isn't, He's correcting your behavior and creating a pure heart within you.

The crucible for silver and the furnace for gold, but people are tested by their praise (Proverbs 27:12)

Can you praise God when things seem to be going all wrong? Explain.

_____

_____

_____

63

Immediately after receiving Jeremiah 29:11, my life seemed to spiral completely out of control. I emailed Elevation Church when they were requesting to hear people testimonies, and encounters with God. I've decide to share my email with you.

Good morning Elevation Team,

My name is Denise Flippen, I'm 32-year-old woman of faith. I titled this email My Incomplete Story because I am currently in a storm, but feeling as though I'll be coming out soon. I began my walk of faith as a Pediatric Nurse and I enjoyed the money and the down time, but honestly it wasn't fulfilling. God not only called me to walk away from the job but my nursing license as well. God has place a purpose in my life. I was call to start an after-school ministry, but the vision didn't stop there. God has place on me a not for profit organization that is going to provide many services to the community, it won't be 501c3 because it's going to be Holy Spirit led. We won't have any stipulations on who, where or how we can help individuals. While pushing forward, the world is crashing down around me. Being a mother of 4 with no job, no home, no vehicle... I left it all behind to follow Jesus and the purpose he has for my life, I find it difficult to keep pushing to live purposefully, but I left my net behind and decided to take a leap of faith, trusting God and his plan for me. Well right now I'm currently in the storm, I do have a after school ministry with 5 consistent young ladies. L.O.V.E. Inc. has become an official not for profit organization acknowledged by the state of NY. LOVE stands for Living Out Victories Every day, and that's exactly what we do... one day at a time. This story is incomplete, but God never starts a work without completing it. I truly trust and believe God in this all because He's the author, alpha and omega, beginning and the end. So, I am yet holding on to faith. I will be in touch and letting you know the outcome. Please pray for and with me for my strength and to continue walking in obedience. Thank for your prayers. To God Be the Glory in ALL we do!!!!

Thanks,

Denise Flippen

Sent from my T-Mobile 4G LTE device

Looking at this letter makes me smile. It was 1 year ago, and God has already created so much change in my life. If it wasn't for my hope that God would provide me a brighter future, I would have given up. And, I wouldn't have been able to say that I am an Author. Just one of the many victories God has in store for me. But, His promise helped me to persevere, and come to know God the way that I do today, and having the desire for other to know Him the same way. My faith will not be shaken, because my roots are planted in the Lord, for the display of His splendor. **(Isaiah 61:3)** Many say it's easy to praise God when everything is all good, then why don't we? We tend to drop God like a bad habit when things are good, but seek Him, or blame Him when they go wrong. Allow God to put your heart in the furnace to purify it, so that you'll be able to praise in Him under any circumstance.

Thank you, Father for giving us hope in you, for the rod of correction that keeps us in check and guiding us to the right path when we are lost. Thank you for giving us hope for a brighter future, not only in Heaven, but success and rewards that are here on earth.

Journal

This week begin to ask God for the purpose for of your life. Take note on how God begins to change the desires of your heart to match His will for your life.

Day1: _____
_____
_____
_____

Day2: _____
_____
_____
_____

Day3: _____
_____
_____
_____

Day4: _____
_____
_____
_____

Day5: _____
_____
_____
_____

Day6: _____
_____
_____
_____

SESSION 13

LOVE ALWAYS PERSEVERES

Persevere, *"continue in a course of action even in the face of difficulty or with little or no prospect of success."* To persevere you must have some sort of hope. We don't stay in a situation that we don't have faith in. I'll share a little secret with you. Right now, as I am writing this book I have a little, what we would call, a crush on someone. We've had small talk and I've left the ball in his court. In all actuality, I'm leaving the ball in God's court. I've prayed about the feelings that I have, and now I'm waiting for God to bring clarity to me regarding the situation. See I choose to love everyone, so connecting love with an emotion is something that I've learned to suppress. I know I feel something, but I want to ensure that what I feel is coming from God. I have been rejected all my life. And, I do not like that feeling. I wrote a poem that I want to share with you.

! Rejected Me!

By: Denise Flippen

As a child, my father continuously rejected me, My mother remarried and he rejected me too...

And for whatever reason, I have a few...

My mother withdrew...

Leaving me feeling empty, lost, hurt and confused...

Because the people I love the most hurt me worse than these dudes do...

So, I adapted a behavior on a long search...

Looking for love from boys, but didn't find much...

When I found Jesus, He wrapped me in His arms...

He promised to He'd never leave me, and never bring me harm...

Now I'm feeling lonely, broken and hurt all at once...

But God is telling me the pain is necessary to learn to pack a punch...

The enemy's always coming, and I can learn to attack him first...

But just in case he hits me good remember Jesus went through worst!!!

Have you ever felt the pain of feeling rejected? Describe the feeling.

_____

_____

_____

Last year on top of all the surrendering of my worldly possessions, God called me to surrender my emotions. This process put my heart into the fire, and I've never experienced pain like it before. When we encounter hurt we typically self- medicate. We turn to drugs, men/women, alcohol, gambling, rage, and/or sports. Anything that will take our mind off the pain. The problem with that is, life is painful. So, we'll forever be looking for a high to suppress the pain we feel, leading to addiction. You have successfully created and idol. God is our comforter. He wants us to lay our burdens at His feet. The things that we run to for comfort have the tendency to destroy our lives and those around us. God restores lives.

The Spirit of the Sovereign Lord is upon me, because the Lord has anointed me to proclaim good news to the poor. He has sent me to bind up the brokenhearted, to proclaim freedom for the captives and release from darkness for the prisoners, to proclaim the year of the Lord's favor and the day of vengeance of our God; to comfort all who mourn, and provide for those who grieve in Zion- to bestow on them a crown of beauty instead of ashes, the oil of joy instead of mourning, and a garment of praise instead of a spirit of despair, They will be called oaks of righteousness, a planting of the Lord for the display of His splendor. They will rebuild the ancient ruins and restore the places long devastated; they will renew the ruined cities that have been devastated for generations. Strangers will shepherd your flocks; foreigners will work your fields and vineyards. And you will be called priests of the Lord, you will be named ministers of our God. You will feed on the wealth of nations, and in their riches, you will boast. Instead of shame you will receive a double portion, and instead

of disgrace you will rejoice in your inheritance. And so, you will inherit a double portion in your land, and everlasting joy will be yours. *"For I the lord loves justice; I hate robbery and wrongdoing in my faithfulness I will reward my people and make an everlasting covenant with them. Their descendants will be known among the nations and their offspring among the peoples. All who see them will acknowledge that they are a people the Lord has blessed."* **I delight greatly in the Lord; my soul rejoices in my God. For He has clothed me with garments of salvation and arrayed me in a robe of His righteousness, as a bridegroom adorns his head like a priest, and as a bride adorns her herself with her jewels. For as the soil makes the sprout come up and a garden causes seeds to grow, so the Sovereign Lord will make righteousness and praise spring up before all the nations.**
(Isaiah 61)

This is my favorite passage in the entire bible. This passage is filled with so much hope, promise and love. How does this passage give you hope?

_____
_____
_____

What's your favorite scripture and why?

_____
_____
_____

I love verse 3 where he describes all our flaws and makes them strengths, and then says that He uses us for His glory. This verse had me googling oak trees to see just how sturdy and beautiful they are. God calls us oak tree, isn't that amazing? The roots of an Oak tree runs deep!

Do you know that this is the prophecy that spoke about the coming of Jesus? This is what Jesus was sent here to do. Jesus read this scripture in a temple and said, *"Prophecy fulfilled."*, sending the religious leaders into a fit of rage, which began their journey to want to take His life. **(Luke 4:17-22)** How powerful is that?

I shared with you last session how I wasn't afraid to died. We'll let me share with you today what I am afraid of, **living! ...** Living requires taking risk, being hurt, feeling rejected, and facing fears. If we're going to get this right we must trust God, His word, and all his promises. My fear of rejection wants to keep me from having hope on this journey of encountering intimacy, but what's fear…False Evidence Appearing Real! I choose to live everyday tearing down false evidence and replacing it with truth. Truth is man may reject me but Jesus deems me valuable! Man, may hurt me, but Jesus will comfort me! All things are working for my good! **I AM FEARFULLY AND WONDERFULLY MADE! These are your truths too!** Knowing these truths will give you the strength you need to persevere. The journey may seem long and hard, but you'll get through it. Make Jesus you best friend, and He'll carry you through it.

What do you think is going to be the most difficult part of this journey?

_____
_____
_____

Now that you wrote them down, tell it to God, He already knows, He's just waiting for you to bring it to Him, so that He may reveal some truths regarding your fears. The Word of God is filled with truths, search it and see for yourself. As for me, I'm going to continue in hope that God will send my husband to me, and that I don't fight or flight when he comes… lol…

Thank you, Father for creating me with hope, and purpose. Thank you for loving me and strengthening me to preserve through any storm just as the mighty oak tree.

Journal

At this point you should be encountering some heart wrenching realities about yourself, while at the same time feeling relieved by the God's truth about who you are. Journal your roller coaster of emotions.

Day1: _____
_____
_____
_____

Day2: _____
_____
_____
_____

Day3: _____
_____
_____
_____

Day4: _____
_____
_____
_____

Day5: _____
_____
_____
_____

Day6: _____
_____
_____
_____

Session 14

Love Never Fails

God is love, and He loves perfectly. How have this study changed your perspective of God, His love for us and how we're called to love others?

_____
_____
_____
_____
_____

Are you walking away feeling more valuable and loved? Explain.

_____
_____
_____
_____
_____

What was the most challenging lesson you've learned these past few sessions? Explain.

_____
_____
_____
_____
_____

What was the most valuable lesson? Explain.

_____
_____

_____

_____

_____

_____

Do you feel that during this study that you have experienced, or have developed a desire to experience the love that this study described?

_____

_____

_____

_____

_____

Don't be shy, tell God how you feel, He's waiting with open arms to receive you. I promise He will not fail you. You have tried it your way long enough, and now you're at a dead end stuck not sure which way to go. Allow God to gently guide you back through your pain, your mess, to get you on the right track. God loves taking a messy situation and turning it into a message. All you must do is say **YES!**

The next step is a simple YES!

You don't have to be in a church or confessing your sins to others. You can do it wherever you are right now. Allow God to make a radical change in your life. Don't hold out until tomorrow, we don't know what today even have in store for us. Just allow God to love you.

I want to close by sharing another poem I wrote during my journey.

Ones Journey to Complete Shalom
Denise Flippen

Contemplated suicide, felt broken, beaten down

Mouth filled with residue from pills while my tears stained the ground

My life was just so miserable feeling really sad

Landed me wanting to die oh so damn bad

Not caring about a heaven, not caring about a hell

My spirit was severely sick and in need of getting well

How did I end up here I was so happy at once in my life?

Or did I suppress how I felt because truly my life has been miserable, filled with pain, rejection, and strife

Empty, worthless, and lost was how I defined myself

The enemy had a seat at my table and he was enjoying himself

But I've found a Savior, one who has given my life a purpose

Stripped me from my worldly gained, and redirected my focus

This journey hasn't been easy, actually quite difficult for me

Because I'm use to buying my lifestyle and paying no attention to the things that are free

This left me feeling empty and all alone

In a room, full of people feeling the need to search my phone

What I was looking for could not be found in man

But in the one who spoke life to create the universe, and proved He loved the world with nails pierced in His hands.

To be continued...

JOURNAL

Use the next few pages to journal freely. It will help relieve some stress by venting. Record your day, your prayers, your doubts, your fears and watch how God works it all together for your good. Be blessed knowing that God loves, you and I love you too!

_____
_____
_____
_____
_____
_____
_____
_____
_____
_____
_____
_____
_____
_____
_____
_____
_____
_____
_____
_____
_____
_____
_____
_____
_____
_____
_____
_____
_____
_____
_____

JOURNAL

READY AIM FIRE

JOURNAL

READY AIM FIRE

JOURNAL

Ready Aim Fire

JOURNAL

Ready Aim Fire

JOURNAL

JOURNAL

Ready Aim Fire

JOURNAL

Ready Aim Fire

JOURNAL

Ready Aim Fire

JOURNAL

Ready Aim Fire

JOURNAL

Ready Aim Fire

JOURNAL

Ready Aim Fire

HELP!!!
Lifestyle of a Worshiper

If you made it this far, it's safe to say that you agree that God's way is the right way and you have decided to give him your

Yes!
Congratulation!!! Welcome to the family.

I must tell you that the next few weeks is going to be packed with tons of information that is going to challenge you a little deeper. Get ready to put your old teachings and tradition to the side as we unpack scriptures and stories in a way that you may have never heard before. I need for you to ask God to fill you up with His Spirit so that you may be able to discern for yourself the truth, and not to simply take my word for it. For many years, people in self-appointed' or man appointed positions have distorted the word of God, most unintentionally, for a lack of understanding, and following tradition. We are going to challenge the stance that is popular amongst most Christian communities, as well as other religions. God is serious about His people and preparing His church for the rise of the Antichrist, which means that Jesus is soon to

RETURN!

SESSION 1

WORSHIP

What is worship?

_____
_____

Worship is defined, *"the expression of, or to show reverence and adoration for a deity."* The bible tells us, "God is spirit, and His worshipers must worship in Spirit and in truth." **(John 4:24)** When we realize the perfect Father that God is, how perfectly He loves us despite our flaws and rebellions, we develop a sincere feeling of gratitude. How do you say, "Thank you."?

What does God want in return for the love that He freely gives to us?

_____
_____
_____

If you studied, **"Love: The Effective Weapon"** then you have a reference of how God loves His children and how we are to love one another. I know, that sounds good in theory, but let's talk about when real life happens. Do you agree with God's way of thinking, and loving? Does loving others this way seems impossible?

Why do you think it's hard to love like God loves?

_____
_____
_____

He's God and He must live in us, to love through us. Well, let's look at a passage from a letter that the Apostle Paul wrote to the church in Rome.

"I do not understand what I do. For what I want to do I do not do, but what I hate I do. And if I do what I do not want to do, I agree that the law is good. As it is, it is no longer I myself who do it, but it is sin living in me. For I know that good itself does not dwell in me, that is, in my sinful nature. For I have the desire to do what is good, but I cannot carry it out. For I do not do the good I want to do, but the evil I do not want to do- this I keep on doing. Now if I do what I do not want to do, it is no longer I who do it, but sin living in me that does it.
(Romans 7:15-20)

So, what Paul is describing is someone who comes into agreement with God, and recognizes that they have been doing this thing wrong. At this point their eyes are open to the fact that they were spiritually dead and is being raised to life. This may weird you out a little, but you'll thank me later. That sin inside of you that the Apostle speaks of, are dark spirits. They are controlling your impulses and causing your actions to be contrary to what you know, and believe. When you give God your **Yes!** you are asking God to come live inside of you. Since light and darkness can't dwell together, when the light moves in, darkness must vacate the premises. But, darkness does not want to go, and will put up a fight. But you have the victory, because your victory was in your **Yes!** Let's look at another passage for conformation.

"If you love me, keep my commands. And I will ask the Father, and He will give you another advocate to help you and be with you forever- the Spirit of truth. The world cannot accept Him, because it neither sees Him nor knows Him. But you know Him, for He lives with you and will be in you. I will not leave you as orphans; I will come to you. Before long, the world will not see me anymore, but you will see me. Because I live, you also live. On that day, you will realize that I am in my Father, and you are in me, and I am in you."
(John 14:15-20)

So, Jesus says if you love me you will keep my command, but also recognizes that it will be difficult, because of what lives in us. We were born into sin, unlike Jesus. Jesus was born with the Spirit of God. He then says, His Father will send us a helper whom He calls, "the Advocate" which will live in us. This is the Spirit that Jesus was born with. I like how Jesus switches up His lingo on us to explain that point. He says, *"I will not leave you as orphans; I will come to you."* Then He says, *"I am in my Father, and you are in me, and I am in you."* So, let's break this down. "The Advocate" is Jesus, but because Jesus is a man, and a man can't literally live in us, the Advocate is His Spirit which is in heaven, in our Father God and in us as well. That's why it is called the Holy Spirit. Because, Jesus has overcome the enemy, by His Spirit, you have also overcome the enemy, because that same Spirit lives in you, once you give Him your **Yes!** Let's look further into scripture to confirm. I want to share 2 scriptures with you.

"You dear children, are from God and have overcome them, because the one who is in you is greater than the one who is in the world."
(1 John 4:4)

Very truly I tell you, whoever believes in me will do the works I have been doing, and they will do even greater things than these, because I am going to the Father. And I will do whatever you ask in my name, so that the Father may be glorified in the Son.
(John 14:12-14)

At this point I want you to discuss all that you have discovered today. If this is challenging for you, share with the group what points are challenging. If this was light and you pretty much understand, share with the group your perspective, and how God helps you. Share techniques with one another. We are our brother's keeper, and must encourage each other on this journey. Next session we will pick up with **(John 14:12-14)**, so be prayerful asking for eyes to see, and ears to hear, to be strengthened in the Spirit to be able to discern truth. I am praying for you all as well.

Journal

Day 1

Day 2

Day 3

Day 4

Day 5

Day 6

SESSION 2

IN THE NAME OF JESUS!

Let's start this session, "In Jesus name!" If you grew up in a Christian home, you were taught to end your prayers, "in Jesus name we pray. Amen." There is power in the name of Jesus. You cast out sickness and demons in the name of Jesus. Have you ever tried doing this? What was your results? If what you expected to happen didn't why do you think that is?

_____
_____
_____
_____
_____

What if the words that came out of your mouth had no power at all? It's not what you said, but where the words came from that lacked the Power? Let's look at a passage of scripture to get a better understanding.

God did extraordinary miracles through Paul so even handkerchiefs and aprons that touched him were taken to the sick, and their illnesses were cured and evil spirits left them. Some Jews who went around driving out evil spirits tried to invoke the name of the Lord Jesus over those who were demon-possessed. They would say, "In the name of Jesus whom Paul preaches, I command you to come out" The Seven sons of Sceva, a Jewish chief priest, were doing this. One day the evil spirit answered them, "Jesus I know, and Paul I know about, but who are you?" Then the man who had the evil spirit jumped on them and overpowered them all. He gave them such a beating that they ran out of the house naked and bleeding.

(Acts 19-11-16)

Ready Aim Fire

So, what do you think went wrong.?

_____

_____

It wasn't a lack of faith, because the word of God says, *"Truly I tell you, if you have faith as small as a mustard seed, you can say to this mountain, 'Move from here to there,' and it will move. Nothing will be impossible for you."* **(Matthew 17:20)** But, what was there faith in? They had faith that the name of Jesus would work and walked around confidently, using the name of Jesus. Their confidence didn't come from nowhere, however; Paul had been performing such miracles as well. What was the difference between the sons of Sceva and Paul?

_____

_____

The issue was that they were trying to mock God, and God cannot be mocked. **(Galatians 6:7)** Using the name of Jesus requires having the authority to use it. Scripture says that, "God performed extraordinary miracles." It's just like being baptized with water. Being baptized with water is an outward expression for man to symbolize what is taking place within you. If you are baptized with water, but is holding back your **Yes!** then you are not baptized with the Holy Spirit. A baptism with the Spirit of God is to allow the Spirt of God to take residence within you. The outward expression is good, but the power lies within.

Peter replied, "Repent and be baptized, every one of you, in the name of Jesus Christ for the forgiveness of your sins. And you will receive the gift of the Holy Spirit."
(Acts 2:38)

Repenting isn't a replacement for the traditional "I'm sorry", You must understand that what you were doing was wrong. It's to agree with God, and to agree to turn from sin. The gift of the Holy Spirit helps you to walk out your repentance to live a life pleasing to God. **Very truly I tell you, whoever believes in me will do the works I have been doing, and they will do even greater things than these, because I am going to the Father. And I will do whatever you ask in my name, so that the Father may be glorified in the Son.**
(John 14:12-14)

Jesus is telling His disciples that the same power that lives in Him will live I them as well. That applies to us also, as sons and daughters of God, baptized with the Holy Spirit. It isn't the words that we say in our own power that moves the mountains, but what we say and do from the Spirit of Jesus that lives within us. But don't go running around trying to cast out demons and laying hands on folks just yet. What you have is similar to a baby Jesus when you first give your **Yes!** Baby Jesus didn't come out of the womb performing miracles, He had to grow into Himself, studying scripture and then coming face to face with temptation and overcoming it. You must feed your spirit just like you feed your body for healthy growth and development. You must go into training in the wilderness, then take and past test in the form of temptations, just like Jesus. We'll dive more into that next session. I will leave you with another passage to get you started.

Finally, be strong in the Lord and in His mighty power. Put on the full armor of God, so that you can take your stand against the devil's schemes. For our struggle is not against flesh and blood, but against the rulers, against the authorities, against the powers of this dark world and against the spiritual forces of evil in the heavenly realm.

(Ephesians 10:12)

Journal

Day 1

_____

_____

_____

_____

_____

_____

_____

_____

_____

_____

_____

_____

_____

_____

Day 2

Day 3

Day 4

Day 5

Day 6

Session 3

The Battle Preparation Plan

I know things are getting tough, and mostly not what you've expected after giving God your **Yes!** Your emotions may be going haywire and everything that could go wrong is starting to. This is typical. What's happening at this point is a few things. One is the enemy is super pissed!!! Yes, I said pissed!!! He is stirring up strife in your life to cause you to want to go back to your settling for less, comfort zone. But, I want you to remember that He can't do anything to you unless God allows him, and if God allows it, it is surely purpose to it. So, as chaos happens in your life, immediately seek God for the lesson. Many of us grew up being told not to question God, but let me clarify this... Questioning God is going to need to be the first thing you do in any circumstance. We need understanding every step of the way, because there's tons of things to learn on this journey.

"Ask and it will be given to you; seek and you will find; knock and the door will be opened to you. For everyone who asks receives; the one who seeks finds; and to the one who knocks, the door will be opened."
(Matthew 7:7-8)

Questioning God, asking God, is scriptural. God doesn't want robots who simply do as He says. He wants us to want to do as He says, because we agree and understand the importance obedience have on our lives. That's why we have free will. He wants us to willingly love Him.

What situation, hurts or disappointments are you facing that you need answers to? Have you asked God? If not try doing so this week. Doing so will allow God into a deep place within you to bring about healing while drawing you closer to Him.

_____
_____
_____

The Battle Preparation Plan

Let's talk a little bit more about this sneaky devil. This week he's going to attempt to attack your mind. He's going to try and convince you that you are unworthy of God's love or of any promises that God had made to you. He will use love ones who with sincere love, will to try to guide you to a different path than the one God has for you, don't be fooled, it may sound like a good thing, but not what God has intended for you. Stay the course and trust the voice of God within you. You may not get the results that you expect, but always look for the lessons. This entire journey is about learning. Learning who God is and who you, truly are. During my journey, I was called delusional several times by my very own mother. It hurt like crazy. There were times I believed it, and went into isolations just wanting to give up, but God wouldn't give up on me. He continued talking to me, and I continued telling Him how I felt, allowing Him in to heal my broken pieces. Keeping this open dialog with God gave me strength to face each day anew. Continue your journey. Your journey is specific to you! Many won't understand, but it's not for them, it's for you!

As the enemy use people, God will do the same. God will send people your direction to give you exactly what you need, to encourage you on this journey. This will be an emotional rollercoaster, lots of tears, and lots of ups and downs. Sometimes all you can do is fight to stay alive, just don't die. Believe me, there will be days that you may want to. Remember this, **"weeping may stay for a night but rejoicing comes in the morning." (Psalms 30:5)** There is a popular saying that is definitely true during this journey, "what doesn't kill you, will make you stronger." Please believe it, and walk in it. Learn the lessons, and apply it.

> **Not that I have already obtained all this, or have already arrived at my goal, but I press on to take hold of that which Christ Jesus took hold of me. Brother's and sister's, I do not consider myself yet to have taken hold of it. But, one thing I do; Forgetting what is behind and straining toward what is ahead, I press on toward the goal to win the prize for which God has called me heavenward in Christ Jesus. (Philippians 3:12-14)**

Paul is referring to not allowing the enemy, we only have one regardless of how he appears, to hold you back form the purpose in which you were created. The reason that Jesus lives in you is to guide you to and through your destiny. You must face the enemy head on an, and attack His lies with God's truth. The enemy knows the truth as well. So often he will tempt you using the word of God, but you must defeat him with the Word. Don't worry about your past, God has that factored into the equation. He's going to use it for His glory. No mess, no message. Next session we will be discussing temptation in more detail, so I want you fully prepared with your armor.

Finally, be strong in the Lord and in His mighty power. Put on the full armor of God, so that you can take your stand against the devil's schemes. For our struggle is not against flesh and blood, but against the rulers, against the authorities, against the powers of this dark world and against the spiritual forces of evil in the heavenly realms. Therefore, put on the full Armor of God, so that when the day of evil comes, you may be able to stand your ground, and after you have done everything, to stand. Stand firm then, with the belt of truth buckled around your waist, with the breastplate of righteousness in place, and with your feet fitted with the readiness that comes from the gospel of peace. In addition to all this take up the shield of faith, with which you can extinguish all the flaming arrows of the evil one. Take the helmet of salvation and the sword of the Spirit, which is the word of God. And pray in the Spirit on all occasions with all kinds of prayers and request. With this in mind, be alert and always keep praying for all the Lord's people.
(Ephesians 6:10-18)

JOURNAL

DAY 1

Day 2

Day 3

Day 4

Day 5

Day 6

SESSION 4
TEMPTATIONS

What is temptation?

_____

What is one of your greatest temptations? What makes it great?

_____

_____

_____

Temptation is defined as, *"a desire to do something, especially something wrong or unwise."* Temptation typically has to do with temporary pleasure or satisfaction. When tempted you usually feel pressured to make an immediate decision, but not always, the enemy also is patient. He knows with the right amount of pressure and time, we are more likely to crack and fall into sin. It is important to keep God's commands on our hearts and lips.

So, what are God's commands?

_____

_____

_____

When most people think of God's commands, the 10 commandments come to mind. While those are God's commands sealed with His finger prints, it's much deeper than that. While the Israelites were in the wilderness God appointed Moses as their leader. Moses was in constant communication with God. God would give Moses instructions for where they were going and how He expected them to behave themselves once they arrived. This is the difference between what we call the Levitical Law, and the 10 Commandment. The Levitical Law were specific to the Israelites, and were established to set them apart from where they came from,

Ready Aim Fire

Egypt. See the Israelites had picked up many of the Egyptians poor behaviors and needed a new identity. The problem with the law was that the Israelites began to simply perform works, but their hearts were far from God because they didn't understand the heart of God, and His intentions for those particular instructions. Because the Israelites heart wasn't in their actions, they began to fall away from the Law, leading them deeper and deeper into sin repeatedly, especially after gaining their promises.

So, how does this relate to us? Can you see yourself in the Israelites shoes? Explain.

_____

_____

_____

The wilderness will be a time to not only learn God, and yourself, but to gain clear instructions as to what He expect specifically from you. After God teaches you, He will also allow you to be tempted. Jesus, a man with no sin had to go through the same process.

Then Jesus was led by the Spirit into the wilderness to be tempted by the devil. After fasting forty days and forty nights, He was hungry. The tempter came to Him and said, "If you are the son of God, tell these stones to become bread." Jesus answered, *"It is written: "Man shall not live on bread alone, but on every word, that comes from the mouth of God.""* **Then the devil took Him to the Holy City and had Him stand on the highest point of the temple. "If you are the Son of God," he said, "throw yourself down for it is written: 'He will command His angels concerning you, and they will lift you up in their hands, so that you will not strike your foot against a stone.'" Jesus answered him,** *"It is also written: Do not put the Lord your God to the test."* **Again, the devil took Him to a very high mountain and showed Him all the kingdoms of the world and their splendor. "All this I will give you," he said, "if you bow down and worship me." Jesus said to him,** *"Away from me Satan! For it is written: "Worship the Lord your God, and serve Him only.""* **Then the devil left Him, and angels came and attended Him.**

It's important to know that before Jesus wound up at this point, He first went through a period of instructions. He learned the scriptures and understood what His father expected from

Him. He could overcome, because He knew who He was and what was in store for Him, post temptation. He had a purpose for life, and He was more dedicated to His purpose rather than His fleshly desires. When the devil tempted Him to eat, His flesh was hungry, but He want to starve the need to please the flesh, and feed His Spirit. He was going to need to be full in the Spirit where He was going, and so will you. The most amazing revelation that God has given me from this passage is the devil tempting Him to fall. This wasn't just any type of fall. This is an attempt to get Jesus to sin. See the bible tells us that we fall, but we can get up. This is true, we fall short and God forgives. While this is true, it is not ok to simply fall expecting God to come to our rescue. When it comes to falling, the fall isn't intentional. Intentionally falling is jumping, and jumping leads to suicide. God is merciful, but His patience does run out, so don't put Him to the test.

How have your thoughts on God's forgiveness led you down the path of sin?

_____

_____

What was the immediate and/or long term effect of your decision to test God?

_____

_____

The enemy's 3rd attempt, Jesus simply dismissed Him. This was easy for Jesus, because the enemy's perspective of success was completely different than that of Jesus. Our perspective of success needs to be to simply live a life pleasing to our Father and walking in our purpose. Hearing "Well done my good and faithful servant."

Journal

Day 1

Day 2

Day 3

Day 4

Day 5

Day 6

Session 5

Eye for an Eye

This session I want to talk about the heart of God, and how He is the same yesterday, today and forevermore. Many people think that God was plain ole evil during Old Testament scriptures and that He became more loving and merciful after Christ.

Do you believe this to be true? Explain.

_____

_____

"If people are fighting and hit a pregnant woman and she gives birth prematurely but there is no serious injury, the offender must be fined whatever the woman's husband demands and the courts allow. But if there is serious injury you are to take life for life, eye for eye, tooth for tooth, hand for hand, foot for foot, burn for burn, wound for wound, bruise for bruise. An owner who knocks out the eye of a male or female slave must let the slave go free to compensate for the eye. And an owner who knocks out the tooth of a male or female slave must let the slave go free to compensate for the tooth."
(Exodus 21:22-27)

"You have heard that it was said, 'Eye for an eye, and tooth for a tooth.' But I tell you, do not resist an evil person. If anyone slaps you on the right cheek, turn to them the other cheek also. And if anyone wants to sue you and take your shirt, hand over your coat as well. If anyone forces you to go one mile, go with them two miles. Give to the one who asks you, and do not turn away from the one who borrows from you.
(Matthew 5:38)

EYE FOR AN EYE

What do you think is the difference between the two judgments given from God? Did God change? Did He become more merciful and forgiving? Explain.

_____

_____

_____

_____

_____

_____

For this reason, He had to be made like them, fully human in every way, in order that He might become a merciful and faithful high priest in service to God, and that He might make atonement for the sins of the people.
(Hebrews 2:17)

God didn't change. He was merciful during both instructions. Jesus came to show us what mercy look like, so that we may extend mercy to each other. The problem was man's lack of understanding God's heart during the initial order. See the commands were given to avoid the fighting between one another, and to hold each one accountable for their actions, taking into consideration each other.

This is what the Lord say: *"Cursed is the one who trusts in man, who draws strength from mere flesh and whose heart turns away from the Lord. That person will be like a bush in the wastelands; they will not see prosperity when it comes. They will dwell in the parched places of the desert, in salt land where no one lives. But, blessed is the one who trust in the Lord, whose confidence is in Him. They will be like a tree planted by the water that sends out its roots by the stream. It does not fear when heat comes' its leaves are always green. It has no worries in a year of drought and never fails to bear fruit. The heart is deceitful above all things and beyond cure. Who can understand it? I the Lord search the heart and examine the mind, to reward each person according to their conduct, according to what their deeds deserve."*
(Jeremiah 17:5-10)

God had allowed man to be the judge between each other and receive vindication at their own hands. The problem was that man's heart turned away from God and began to draw strength from pleasing their flesh rather than pleasing God. This brought about a lot of bloodshed. This was not a representation of the heart of God at all. Jesus came to take the power from the devil and to give it back for us to use only through His Spirit. We no longer have the right to bring bout judgment, because it's done from a sinful, deceitful nature. But, God is pure in love and able to judge according to the heart. He sees the motive behind all deeds, good and bad, and can reward or punish accordingly. So, Jesus tells us, since we couldn't get it right with living to please God and maintaining a heart toward Him, He will walk it out for us. This doesn't mean that we don't have to live it, but we have an example of God's heart, and intent for the law. So, let's clear this up, Jesus didn't come here for God to understand us, but for us to understand Him!

"Do not think I have come to abolish the Law or the Prophets; I have not come to abolish them but to fulfill them. For truly I tell you, until heaven and earth disappear, not the smallest letter, not the least stroke of a pen, will by any means disappear from the Law until everything is accomplished. Therefore, anyone who sets aside one of the least of these commands and teaches others' accordingly will be called least in the kingdom of heaven, but whoever practices and teaches these commands will be called great in the kingdom of heaven. For I tell you that unless your righteousness surpasses that of the Pharisees and the teachers of the law, you will certainly not enter the kingdom of heaven. **(Matthew 5:17-20)**

The sermon on the mount is a great representation of how God commands us to live, taught by Jesus Himself. I am praying for you all to be strengthened with strength to continue moving forward in living a life pleasing to God. The beginning it tough, but having a support system who's on the journey with you and dedicated to walking into their destiny, will help give you the push needed. Never the less, God is sufficient and will send his messengers, and provide you with the strength needed to continue.

Journal

Day 1

Day 2

Day 3

Day 4

Day 5

Day 6

Session 6

Jesus vs. The Pharisees

"Listen to another parable: There was a landowner who planted a vineyard. He put a wall around it, dug a winepress in it and built a watch tower. Then he rented the vineyard to some farmers and moved to another place. When the harvest time approached, he sent his servants to the tenants to collect his fruit. The tenants seized his servants; they beat one killed another and stoned a third. Then he sent other servants to them, more than the first time. And the tenants treated them the same way. Last of all, he sent his son to them. 'They will respect my son,' he said. But when the tenants saw the son, they said to each other, 'This is the heir. Come, let's kill him and take his inheritance.' So, they took him and threw him out of the vineyard and killed him. Therefore, when the owner of the vineyard comes, what will he do to those tenants?" **"He will bring those wretches to a wretched end," they replied, "and he will rent the vineyard to other tenants, who will give him his share of the crop at harvest time."** *Jesus said to them, "Have you never read in the Scriptures: 'The stone the builders rejected has become the cornerstone; the lord has done this, and it is marvelous in our eyes'? Therefore, I tell you that the kingdom of God will be taken away from you and given to a people who will produce its fruit. Anyone who falls on this stone will be broken into pieces; anyone on whom it falls will be crushed."* **When the chief priests and the Pharisees heard Jesus' parables, they knew he was talking about them. They looked for a way to arrest Him, but they were afraid of the crowd because the people held that He was a prophet.**
(Matthew 21:33-46)

Have you ever overheard someone having a conversation, they were talking about someone but they mentioned no names? Have you ever assumed they were talking about you? Why did you assume they were talking about you?

_____

Usually when we assume a conversation is about us, it is because the conversation has some truth to it. How did the conversation make you feel? What was your response and why?

_____
_____
_____
_____
_____

This was the Pharisees problem. They could see themselves in the parable. Jesus was calling them out, and they didn't like it. The Pharisees were the big dogs in town and Jesus challenged their status, their position, and they couldn't have that. They only had themselves in mind. For centuries, the Jews had been God's chosen people, but instead of treating others with respect and love, the way God treated them, they oppressed and trample others. They were reaping benefits but not sharing with other, specifically not God. Their heads had gotten big, full of hot air.

If I speak in tongues of men or of angels, but do not have love, I am only a resounding gong or a clanging cymbal. If I have the gift of prophecy and can fathom all mysteries and all knowledge, and if I have a faith that can move mountains, but do not have love, I am nothing. If I give all I possess to the poor and give over my body to hardship that I may boast, but do not have love, I gain nothing.
(1 Corinthians 13:1-3)

For God's gifts and His call are irrevocable. Just as you who were at one time disobedient to God have now received mercy as a result of their disobedience, so they too have now become disobedient in order that they too may now receive mercy as a result of God's mercy to you. For God has bound everyone over to disobedience so that He may have mercy on them all.
(Romans 11:29-32)

We are born with our gifts, we don't need to repent to preform or to walk in our gifts, but we will not have the peace, power, and joy that comes with walking in God's righteousness while operating in our gifts. 1 Corinthians says you are nothing, and you profit nothing. Money, fame and worldly possessions are nothing, when you have lost yourself. The Pharisees had a false sense of self, attached to their fame.

How do you think they got this way?

_____

_____

_____

They had developed a fear for God instead of reverence. They're two different things. They were aware of the consequences that their ancestors faced due to their disobedience. So, they feared that if their disobedience was exposed, they would receive a rebuking from the prophets. The Israelites didn't take responsibility for their actions, but pointed the finger at the Prophets who spoke the disappointments of God, and delivered the message of chastisement. We shouldn't fear chastisement, but welcome it, because it teaches us what's wrong and corrects us. Fear hardens your heart driving you deeper into sin, and ultimately into pride.

My son, do not despise the Lord's discipline, and do not resent His rebuke, because the Lord discipline those He loves, as a father the son he delights in.
(Proverbs 3 11-12)

I want to encourage you to read the book of proverbs one chapter at a time, allowing God to speak to you through His word. Proverbs is full of knowledge and wisdom. The Spirit within you, once fed, will assist you in applying what you learned.

Journal

Day 1

Day 2

Day 3

Day 4

Day 5

Day 6

SESSION 7
WHAT'S YOUR ENDING?

We must pay the most careful attention, therefore, to what we have heard, so that we do not drift away. For since the message spoken through angels was binding, and disobedience received its just punishment, how shall we escape if we ignore so great a salvation? This salvation which was first announced by the Lord, was confirmed to us by those who heard Him. God also testified to it by signs, wonders and miracles, and by gifts of the Holy Spirit distributed according to His will. It is not to angels that He has subjected the world to come, about which we are speaking. But, there is a place where someone has testified: "What is mankind that you are so mindful of them, a Son of man that you care for Him? You made them a little lower than the angels; you crowned them with glory and honor and put everything under their feet." In putting everything under them, God left nothing that is not subject to them. Yet at present we do not see everything subject to them. But we do see Jesus, who was made lower than the angels for a little while, now crowned with glory and honor because He suffered death, so that by the grace of God He might taste death for everyone. In bringing many sons and daughters to glory, it was fitting that God, for whom and through whom everything exists, should make the pioneer of their salvation perfect through what He suffered. Both the one who makes people holy and those who are made holy are of the same family. So, Jesus is not ashamed to call them brothers and sisters. He says, *"I will declare your name to my brothers and sisters; in the assembly I, will sing your praises."* And again, *"I will put my trust in him."* And again, He says, *"Here am I, and the children God has given me."* Since the children have flesh and blood, He too share in their humanity so that by His death He might break the power of him who holds death- that is, the devil- and free those who all their lives were held in slavery by their fear of death. For surely it is not angels He helps, but Abraham's descendants. For this reason, He had to be made like them, fully human in every way, in order that

He might become a merciful and faithful high priest in service to God, and that He might make atonement for the sins of the people. Because He Himself suffered when He was tempted, He is able to help those who are being tempted.
(Hebrews 2:1-18)

I like to say, 'If we miss the fact that Jesus was fully human, then we miss it all, and if we miss the fact that He is God we miss it all as well." We must be able to look at Jesus with both eyes, to gain an understanding of His purpose. In His humanity with the Spirit of God dwelling in Him from birth, He walked out this life perfectly. This is something man can never do, because we are born into sin. But, once we allow the Spirit of God to be made perfect in us, we then have the power to live as Jesus did.

There is no difference between Jew and Gentile, for all have sinned and fall short of the glory of short of the glory of God.
(Romans 3:22-23)

What does this scripture mean to you?

_____
_____
_____

Most people use this scripture as their license to sin and it's not at all. "Have" is used in the past tense. None of us are born with the Spirit of God. But, once we agree with God and accept the Holy Spirit to reside within us, we are commanded to be obedient to our Spirit. The spirit of the evil one will continue to tempt you for the rest of your natural life, but Jesus died for your victory, all you have to do is walk in it.

No temptation has overtaken you except what is common to mankind And God is faithful; He will not let you be tempted beyond what you can bear. But, when you are tempted, He will also provide a way out so that you can endure it.
(1 Corinthians 10:13)

God does His part but we must do ours as well. It's a partnership. A relationship. He wants us to be willing participants. We must know and understand that God has our best interest at heart always, every step of the way.

"Father, if you are willing, take this cup from me; yet not my will, but yours be done."
An angel appeared to Him and strengthened Him.

Jesus was human and became weak and wanted to make an escape, but He knew God had His best interest at heart, and He trusted Him. Because, of His obedience, love, sacrifice and dedication to His father's will, we now are co-heirs. Aren't you thankful?! Now we get to join in on the promises of Jesus. Let's look at what Jesus promised His disciples.

A dispute also arose among them as to which of them was considered to be the greatest. Jesus said to them, *"The king of the Gentiles lord it over them; and those who exercise authority over them call themselves Benefactors. But, you are not like that. Instead, the greatest among you should be like the youngest, and the one who serves. For who is the greater, the one who is at the table or the one who serves? Is it not the one who is at the table? But, I am among you as one who serves. You are those who have stood by me in my trials. And I confer on you a kingdom, just as my Father conferred one on me, so that you may eat and drink at my table in my kingdom and sit on thrones, judging the twelve tribes of Israel. Simon, Simon, Satan has asked to shift you all as wheat. But, I have prayed for you, Simon, that your faith may not fail. And when you have turned back, strengthen your brothers."*
(Luke 22:24-32)

Who wants to feast at the table with Jesus? I know I do. To finally live in true Holy Majesty. It gets no better than that!

Now replace Simon with your name. We have the same promise. Simon fell, but He got up and strengthen his brothers. Who's waiting to borrow strength from you?

Journal

Day 1

Day 2

Day 3

Day 4

Day 5

Day 6

Hello...
Fasting on the Other Side

It's a beautiful feeling to see the sunlight after living in darkness for so long. The journey of being made new is very heavy, and seems like true long suffering, but I tell you, "Weeping endures for a night, but joy comes in the morning." I'll tell you, that's an accurate scripture and popular saying, and it's true. It's true while your crying every night due to a stir of emotions, and it's also true once you have been made into the person God intended for you to be. The most difficult process is getting rid of old habits and learning to apply new ones. After we become whole, and the breaking process is complete, God begin to use us in ways we never knew was possible. You will discover that there are truly seeds of greatness within you that you never knew existed. God will use you in ways you have never imagined. Are you ready to get started?

Well...

Welcome to the other side!

Notes:

Session 1

Fasting

Fasting is an essential part of a relationship with God. Fasting is to starve your natural fleshy desires, while feeding and tending to your spiritual needs. It is how we make a sacrifice to God, and obtain a variety of things in return. We'll discuss different fast that occurred in scripture, and see why and how they were carried out. Remember that God is the one who calls the fast, and will let you know what He's requesting from you.

While you were in the wilderness God called for you to give up many things. Many of those things needed to go, because they had no place in your life. There are many things on earth that are for our enjoyment. Sometimes, we take so much enjoyment in these things, that they have the potential to become idols, if they weren't. They had the potential to distract you from where you are going, or to feed your mind with the lies that the enemy tells us. So, we must learn to let them go, and resist our natural desire to please our flesh, rather than pleasing God. There were a few things, that God called me to give up in the wilderness that I could pick back up on this side, but I had to become a new person to learn how to enjoy those things appropriately. So, let's clear this up, living a life pleasing to God is not boring. It appears that way when people are afraid to live, everything you have put down is not permanently, and somethings are. Let God direct you, He will make it very clear to you.

This series we have a basic go to scripture.

Do not deprive each other except perhaps by mutual consent and for a time, so that you may devote yourselves to prayer. Then come together again so that Satan will not tempt you because of your lack of self-control.
(1 Corinthians 7:5)

This is simple advice that the Apostle Paul is giving us pertaining to sex in marriage. Can we agree that sex is an act that we participate in to please our flesh? Most people look at sex as this thing that is simply wrong or nasty. Sex is beautiful, but utilized in the context outside of the way God ordained, is dangerous. It has become normal to simply please our flesh regardless of the consequences attached to it. This lust leads us into all sorts of unnecessary destruction. Not only physically, but emotionally, and spiritually as well. But, God doesn't want us afraid of sex, He wants us to enjoy sex, but within the context in which He has created it.

Then the Lord taken the woman from the rib He had taken out of the man, and He brought it to him. The man said, "this is now bone of my bones and flesh of my flesh; she shall be called 'woman,' for she was taken out of mam." That is why a man leaves his father and mother and is united to his wife, and they become one flesh. Adam and his wife were both naked, and they felt no shame.

(Genesis 2:22-25)

The desire we have be one with someone is natural. A woman came from a man and longs to return where she belongs. This is natural. Man, is born of a woman so, it's natural for him to feel the same, besides once again, originally, she came from him. We tend to feel as if something is missing. Even after you have allowed God to make you whole, and He feels your voids, the longing feeling still exist, because there is a missing piece. God holds it, and when it's time, He will give it to you. Many don't believe that there is only one specific person for you, but I disagree. God says that He has the perfect will for our lives, and I believe that across the board. Scripture says, "man leaves his father and mother and is united with **"his"** wife," not **"a"** wife. So, any old wife or husband won't do, but the one that God destined for you. We must be walking in His will to know without a doubt if the one we're joined with is from God. We run around in sin all our lives attaching ourselves to things that we have no business being attached to. Then, we are upset when those things must be broken. No God is not pleased with divorce, but God is not pleased to see His children attached to things we had no business attached to in the first place either. There are consequences regardless. Remaining bound to, or in situations, or relationships God didn't ordain is bondage, and self-abuse. You don't have to live in misery. Yes, divorce is sin, and there will be chastisement, but the Lord chastise those He loves. Discipline is necessary to correct us when we fall short, to assist us in changing the behavior, so that we don't find ourselves in the same situation again. We are to be married to Christ, but first we need to divorce the enemy, shaking loose the bondage he had us trapped in. By no means am I saying if things aren't going well in your marriage, run get a divorce, what I am saying is that you must seek Good about it, and do what He instructs you to do regardless of what people may say. Don't remain in ungodly circumstances for appearances, and fear of shame, or judgement from man. There is a difference in chastisement and abuse. Accept your consequences and move on with the lessons learned, ensuring not to continue circling that mountain.

If you are single and have a desire to have sex, maybe you're a virgin holding out for marriage, or maybe you are turning a new leaf of celibacy in your life, and have now decided to abstain until marriage, talk to someone who has already been there and can give you pointers on how they overcame the temptations. I can tell you this, for me it has been 1 ½ years, and God has not only taught me why it was wrong, and gave me hope for a future, but He has always provided an escape when temptation seemed great. You must face your temptations and not run from it. Knowing your strength and weakness are key. Your desire to please God must be stronger than your desire to please your flesh! Here's a scripture that also came in handy for my journey.

Do you not know that your bodies are members of Christ Himself? Shall I then take the members of Christ and unite them with a prostitute? Never! Do you not know that he who unites himself with a prostitute is one with her in body? For it is said, "The two will become one flesh." But whoever is united with the Lord is one with Him in spirit. Flee from sexual immorality. All other sins a person commits are outside the body, but whoever sins sexually, sins against their own body. Do you not know that your bodies are temples of the Holy Spirit, who is in you, whom you have received from God? You are not your own; you were bought at a price. Therefore, honor God with your bodies.
(1 Corinthians 6:15-20)

Once I asked God to live in me, my body became a temple. God goes where I go, and is a part of what I'm a part of. I can't just separate from Him for a moment, or put Him down for a second, He lives in me. I don't want to subject God to such dishonor. This way of thinking helped me greatly. Please don't be scared to share your truth with other. You never know who is going through a challenging time, and need to hear your testimony.

Furthermore; we are married to God, and adultery is a sin that brings about destruction. Adultery is not only about physical marriage, but we need to take our marriage to God very seriously.

> **But a man who commits adultery has no sense; whoever does so destroy himself.**
> **(Proverbs6:32)**

> *"I the lord search the heart and examine the mind, to reward each person according to their conduct, according to what their deeds deserve."*
> **(Jerimiah 17:10)**

We cannot fool God with our works, He looks directly at the heart. If your heart is right, then your actions will follow your heart. Adultery begins in the mind and takes root in the heart.

> **Above all else, guard your heart, for everything you do flows from it. Keep your mouth free of perversity; keep corrupt talk far from your lips. Let your eyes look straight ahead; fix your gaze directly before you. Give careful thought to the paths for your feet and be steadfast in all your ways. Do not turn from the right or the left; keep your foot from evil.**
> **(Proverbs 4:23-27)**

This scripture is every important once you make it to this side. The wilderness was difficult because you went through many phases allowing God to clean up your heart. It hurt, didn't it? But, it was worth the changes God made within you. Nobody wants to go through that pain again. Well, then you mustn't allow sin to creep back in, and make your heart it's home. Keep your eyes fixed on God. Like we learned in *"Love: The Effective Weapon,"* we guard our hearts by loving freely allowing God to guard it. We also learned that the path to adultery is very appealing and tempting. It is sticky and slippery business, once you began to play with it you get caught up before you even know it. Satan is very manipulative. So, keep your eyes focused on God and watch your step, ensuring not to fall into a trap. And in case of a fall, don't stay there, you must get right back up! God loves you still!!!

Notes:

SESSION 2

3 DAY FAST

I like to call the 3 day fast, "the death and resurrection fast." This fast is when you have nothing to eat or drink at all, sometimes, you'll drink only water. You are dying to your flesh, while feeding your Spirit. Let's pull up the scripture from 1 Corinthians again today.

Do not deprive each other except perhaps by mutual consent and for a time, so that you may devote yourselves to prayer. Then come together again so that Satan will not tempt you because of your lack of self-control.
(1 Corinthians 7:5)

Remember we are married to God first. The type of fast that you are going to participate in should come from God. You may feel like you want to fast during a certain time, but there must be a mutual consent. You must understand why you are fasting. What do you expect out of your fast? If God isn't in agreement with your decision to fast you won't have the strength to complete it. Let's look at a story of a 3 day fast in scripture.

When Mordecai learned of all that had been done, he tore his clothes, put on sackcloth and ashes, and went out into the city, wailing loudly and bitterly. But he went only as far as the king's gate, because no one clothed in sackcloth was allowed to enter it. In every province to which the edict and order of the king came, there was great mourning among the Jews, with fasting, weeping and wailing. Many lay in sackcloth and ashes. When Esther's eunuchs and female attendants came, and told her about Mordecai, she was in distress. She sent clothes for him to put on instead of his sackcloth, but he would not accept them. Then Esther summoned Hathak, one of the king's eunuchs assigned to attend her, and ordered him to find out what was troubling Mordecai and why. So, Hathak went out to Mordecai in the open square of the city in front of the king's gate. Mordecai told him everything that had happened to

3 Day Fast

him, including the exact amount of money Haman had promised to pay into the royal treasury for the destruction of the Jews. He also gave him a copy of the edict for their annihilation, which has been published in Susa, to show Esther and explained it to her, and to go into the king's presence to beg for mercy and plead with him for her people. Hathak went back and reported to Esther what Mordecai had said. Then she instructed him to say to Mordecai, "All the king's officials and the people of the royal provinces know that for any man or woman who approaches the king in the inner court without being summonsed the king has a law: that they be put to death unless the king extends the gold scepter to them and spares their lives. But thirty days have passed since I was called to go to the king." When Esther's words were reported to Mordecai, he sent back this answer: "Do not think that because you are in the king's house you alone of all the Jews will escape. For if you remain silent at his time, relief and deliverance for the Jews will arise from another place, but you and your father's family will perish. And who knows but that you have come to your royal position for such a time as this?" Then Esther sent this reply to Mordecai: "Go gather together all the Jews who are in Susa, and fast for me. Do not eat or drink for three days, night or day. I and my attendants will fast as you do. When this is done, I will go to the king, even though it is against the law. And if I perish, I perish." So, Mordecai went away and carried out all of Esther's instructions.

(Esther 4:1-17)

I remember when God called me to my first 3 day fast. He told me, "Fast like your life depends on it." At that time, I wasn't familiar with this here story. At the end of my fast I came face to face with the enemy. He was bent on trying to shake me up. He wanted to scare me into giving up my life of destiny. He wanted a Spiritual death. I thank God that He prepared me for that day, because I entered the battle field strong, standing firm, and ready for war. I overcame that devil that day. Because, I was strengthened in my Spirit, I could look that devil in the face and have him bow out to the power of God that lives in me. That was a scary, but more so an amazing experience. God showed me very clearly who I am, because He lives in me.

Esther requested her people to partake in this 3-day fast, because of what she had been called to do could very well cost her life. The Jews life was already on the line, and the only one who could stop the annihilation of the Jews was the king. Although she was his wife, she couldn't just enter his presence, doing so could be suicide. Esther, and all who had been called to fast, were fasting for Esther to have the strength to face death and to overcome it.

I call this fast the death and resurrection fast, because Jesus fleshed died and in three days He was resurrected defeating death and overcoming it. He walked into His Glory. Victory was on the other side, and He made it. Just like Esther. If you continue reading the story, Esther approached the king with boldness, and not only did he spared her life, but the life of all the Jews. He also defeated and reigned down judgement on their enemies.

The last time God called me to a three day fast, He simply said, "Where I'm taking you your flesh can't go." He was telling me great temptation is coming my way, and that I must be prepared to walk away from it regardless how heavy or good it may feel to me. I thank God for the fast, because I feel stronger and empowered to say NO! when it comes.

If God is calling you to a 3-day fast, fear not, you can do it. Don't worry about health concerns, God has that figured out. If He calls you to it, He will strengthen you, and bring you through it!

Notes:

SESSION 3

10 DAY FAST

This session we are going to look at a passage in the book of Daniel. But, first we'll refresh our minds with our signature verse.

Do not deprive each other except perhaps by mutual consent and for a time, so that you may devote yourselves to prayer. Then come together again so that Satan will not tempt you because of your lack of self-control.
(1 Corinthians 7:5)

During our fasting times, we must remember that we are to be submitting ourselves to prayer. Prayer is communication with God. We are called to pray consistently. We talk to Him, He talks to us, using all our senses especially hearing and sight. We often speak to God, but not often do we wait for a response. It's as if God is just this superior being that we can just dump on, and not to expect anything in return. God has much that He want to share with us as well, we must be willing to receive. There is so much knowledge in Christ, and He's just waiting for individuals that He can dump it into! Are you willing?

Then the king ordered Ashpenaz, chief of his court officials, to bring into the king's service some of the Israelites from the royal family and nobility- young men without any physical defect, handsome, showing aptitude for every kind of learning, well informed, quick to understand, and qualified to serve in the king's palace. He was to teach them the language and literature of the Babylonians. The king assigned them a daily amount of food and wine from the king's table. They were to be trained for three years, and after that they were to enter the king's service. Among those who were chosen were some from Judah: Daniel, Hananiah, Mishael and Azariah. The chief official gave them new names: Daniel, the name Belteshazzar; to Hananiah, Shadrach; to Mishael, Meshach; and to Azariah, Abednego. But, Daniel resolved not to defile himself with

the royal food or wine, and he asked the chief official for permission not to defile himself this way. Now God had caused the official to show favor and compassion to Daniel, but the official told Daniel, "I am afraid of my lord the king, who has assigned your food and drink. Why should he see you looking worse than the other young men your age? The king would then have my head because of you." Daniel then said to the guard whom the chief official had appointed over Daniel, Hananiah, Mishael and Azariah, "Please test your servants for ten days: Give us nothing but vegetables to eat and water to drink. Then compare our appearance with that of the young men who eat the royal food, and treat your servants in accordance with what you see." So, he agreed to this and tested them for ten days. At the end of the ten days they looked healthier and better nourished than any of the young men who ate the royal food. So, the guard took away their choice food and the wine they were to drink and gave them vegetables instead. To these four young men God gave knowledge and understanding of all kinds of literature and learning. And Daniel could understand dreams of all kinds. At the end of the time set by the king to bring them into his service, the chief official presented them to Nebuchadnezzar. The king talked with them, and he found none equal to Daniel, Hananiah, Mishael and Azariah; so, they entered the king's service. In every matter of wisdom and understanding about which the king questioned them, he found them ten times better than all the magicians and enchanters in his whole kingdom. And Daniel remained there until the first year of King Cyrus.

(Daniel 1:1-21)

This is so amazing to me. The world has its ways to gain strength, knowledge and success, but God has a way all of His own. Please listen to me when I say this. God qualifies the unqualified. You do not need the accolades of the world to accomplish the thing in which God has called you. I have never attended seminar, nor have I trained under any official, of any sort. I have been asked where do I get my knowledge, and I must honestly say the Holy Spirit teaches me, and He is truly the best instructor. While putting together this book the enemy tried to attack my mind with doubts of my capability, and credentials to write and publish such a book. He tried telling me who I wasn't, and comparing me with other authors. I reminded him who I was, and that I didn't write the book in the first place, the Spirit within me did! That shut him up, but only for a moment. He later returned with doubt that anyone would read it, and if they did, the pastors that I look up to would disagree with my use of scripture and passages. I told that devil, seeing that I didn't use the scriptures, heck, most of the scriptures I used I looked at differently or never heard of them before writing the book. It wouldn't be me they're rejecting, but God himself. Lastly, he simply tried distracting me with the one thing I desire deeply… Intimacy. God refocused me immediately.

I felt God calling me into a fast the 1st of January and because everyone everywhere was doing the 21 day fast, which we'll discussed next session, I thought I was fasting 21 days. God had me to seek him, and His word. I shortly realized that God was calling me to a 10 day fast. During that time, God showed me my weakness with how I eat. He gave me a new way of eating that will not only assist me with weight lost, but to live longer as well. It's not about a diet, but a lifestyle change. The only way to live this life is to understand why the change is necessary. God will do that for you. You must first seek Him for the knowledge. You only need to sacrifice that thing that God is requesting from you, and He will feed you knowledge that will change your life.

Notes:

Session 4

21 Day Fast

If there was a way for me to write this book, and give it away for free I honestly would. God gave me this vision, and I had a tough time accepting it. I want to freely give away what God shares with me. I trust God as my provider, and as I'm writing this chapter the enemy tried me again with a foreclosure notice. I laughed, because he's trying very hard to break me. Last year it would've worked. I would've went into deep depression, crying all crazy and asking God why He's leading me down this path. I would've thought I wasn't strong enough to complete this journey, and would have begged for death. I would've sworn God was against me. I heard God very clearly when he told me to walk away from everything including my nursing job. I heard Him very clearly when He said nothing my hands could do. My life began falling apart, and I only had hope to hold me up. I trust God, and His promises. I've gained so much insight within a year. I know God like I never have, ever in my life. I hold everything loosely, and if I must give up my house… I will! So, this foreclosure letter didn't scare me. I don't like it, but I don't fear it. And I still want millions of people to get this book, and if it could be for free, that would be amazing. There is no limit on the price I would pay for others to experience the love, and knowledge of Christ that I have gained. That leads me to my second point.

Unlike so many, we do not peddle the word of God for profit. On the contrary, in Christ we speak before God with sincerity, as those sent from God.
(2 Corinthians 2:17)

The 21 day fast has been turned into a popular diet, and the 21 day fast is absolutely NOT a diet. Many have profited by turning this fast into a trendy new year resolution to lose weight. There are many books, and fitness equipment that is using the Daniel plan to sell their products.

21 Day Fast

Let's look to scripture to get a true understanding of the heart and purpose of Daniel's 21 day fast. First, let's checkout our 1 Corinthians scripture.

Do not deprive each other except perhaps by mutual consent and for a time, so that you may devote yourselves to prayer. Then come together again so that Satan will not tempt you because of your lack of self-control.
(1 Corinthians 7:5)

When we call, ourselves participating in a fast, God not only instructs us on purpose, and time, He also strengths us during the fast and give us strength for the temptation that comes after the fast. How many times have you participated in a diet, only not to have the strength to complete, but once you returned to your regular way of eating, gaining all your weight back. You go without a certain food group for so long that when your free to return, you indulged. I'm talking about straight gluttony. It's very common. Daniel's 21 day fast had nothing to do with weight loss. Let's peek at what scripture says.

In the third year of Cyrus king of Persia, a revelation was given to Daniel (who was called Belteshazzar). Its message was true and it concerned a great war. The understanding of the message came to him in a vision. At that time, I, Daniel, mourned for three weeks. I ate no choice food; no meat or wine touched my lips; and I used no lotions at all until the three weeks were over. On the twenty-fourth day of the first month, as I was standing on the bank of the great river, the Tigris, I looked up and there before me was a man dressed in linen, with a belt if fine gold from Uphaz around his waist. His body was like topaz, his face like lightening, his eyes like flaming torches, his arms and legs like the gleam of burnished bronze, and his voice like the sound of a multitude. I, Daniel, was the only one who saw the vision; those who were with me did not see it, but such terror overwhelmed them that they fled and hid themselves. So, I was left alone, gazing at this great vision; I had no strength left, my face turned deathly pale and I was helpless. Then I heard him speaking, I fell into a deep sleep, my face to the ground. A hand touched me and set me trembling on my hands and knees. He said, *"Daniel, you who are highly esteemed, consider carefully the words I am about to say to you, and stand up, for I have now been sent to you."* And when he

said this to me, I stood up trembling. Then he continued, *"Do not be afraid, Daniel. Since the first day that you set your mind to gain understanding and to humble yourself before your God, your words were heard, and I have come in response to them. But the prince of the Persian kingdom resisted me twenty-one days. Then Michael, one of the chief princes, came to help me, because I was detained there with the king of Persia. Now I have come to explain to you what will happen to your people in the future, for the vision concerns a time yet to come."* **While He was saying this to me, I bowed with my face toward the ground and was speechless. The one who looked like a man touched my lips, and I opened my mouth and began to speak. I said to the one standing before me, "I am overcome with anguish because of the vision, my Lord, and I feel very weak. How can I, your servant, talk with you, my Lord? My strength is gone and I can hardly breathe." Again, the one who looked like a man touched me and gave me strength.** *"Do not be afraid, you who are highly esteemed,"* **He said.** *"Peace! Be strong now; be strong."* **When He spoke to me, I was strengthened and said, "Speak, my Lord, since you have given me strength."** **He said,** *"Do you know why I have come to you? Soon I will return to fight against the prince of Persia, and when I go, the prince of Greece will come; but first I will tell you what is written in the Book of Truth. (No one supports me against them except Michael, your prince.*

(Daniel 10:1-21)

Sorry to leave you hanging right there… lol… But you can continue to chapter 11 if you choose. That was enough information to drive this point home. First key point, Daniel's emotional distress, and concern lead him to the fast. He was in a place of "anguish" says scripture. Daniel had had a vision and it didn't sit well with him. The Lord came to Daniel to explain to Him what was about to occur.

Secondly, Daniel fast wasn't clear. Scripture began by saying he ate no **"choice"** food for 3 weeks. Meat and wine happen to be the choice food for him during that time. It has nothing to do with health or weight loss. He was simply denying himself; a sacrifice, to receive insight from God as to what he should be doing, if anything. God allowed him to see these things, which indicates instructions are needed. We don't just have visions for no reason. If God gave you a vision, ask for clarity, but don't be shocked if you end up fasting. Embrace the journey.

Third, when the Lord appeared before Daniel, he became deathly weak. It wasn't because of the fast, but because of the presence of God, and God filled him up with strength. When fasting, it is important that we are seeking God above all else. That is where our strength come from. Not from man! Once again if God called you to it he will strengthen you through it. He will also give you the strength to combat the temptation that follows. You don't have to fast meat or carbs, but seek God as to what He will have you to give up, He will show you.

Lastly, if you treat this fast like a diet, you will miss the main point. Your mind will be so wrapped up on the way you are supposed to eat, counting calories, looking at labels and watching the scale, that you will miss the voice of God if He decides to whisper in the wind. We must not treat fasting like a diet, because it absolutely is not!

I began doing the 21-day diet/fast in January when God informed me that, that's not the way to fast. He then gave me knowledge on how He wanted me to eat, and what fasting was all about. In February, when it became time for me to fast for 21 days, I was still a little messed up, and overwhelmed about what I had to give up. I made it so complex that that's all I could think of. God quickly simplified it for me. He choice my food, as well as Facebook, and some friendships that had consumed me emotionally and timely. My friend understood. During that time, He was dealing with some things she had going on as well. She need a break from hearing my voice, to hear God clearly. The last week of my fast was when God gave me instructions to write this book.

This book has been an amazing journey for me. I was taught, and challenged frequently. It was very eye opening, and convicting at times. I pray that it challenges your perspective as much as it has challenged mines.

The Lord bless you and keep you; the Lord make His face shine on you and be gracious to you; the Lord turn his face toward you and give you peace!
(Numbers 6:24-26)

Notes:

Final Thoughts!!!

We have come to a close, and some amazing things has happened in my life between the time I have started this book, and now. I will save that info for a later date. Just know that God is nothing short of amazing. I'm sure you guys have some amazing testimonies as well. I would love to hear some of you guy's stories, and receive feedback from the lessons you've learned. I don't have a website set up yet, but you may reach me on Facebook. My name on Facebook is Denise Flippen, and I have a Facebook page Living Out Victories Every Day. Feel free to message me, and I will respond as I am available.

During your journey, I know God has severed some relationships. Some are permanent, others will be restored, however; God promises not to leave us as orphans. This is not limited to the Holy Spirit that accompanies us on this journey, but the family He gives us as heirs to the kingdom. If you haven't already, I am praying for God to place you in a church home designated specifically to meet your spiritual, and emotional need. God will also provide for you physical, don't fret. He cares about it all.

I have provided 30 extra pages for journaling, please use them. Writing out your feelings, and prayers will help greatly as a visual for your experiences. You will be able to look back, and see the hand of God over your life. May God bless you all!!!

Journal

JOURNAL

Ready Aim Fire

JOURNAL

Journal

JOURNAL

JOURNAL

Ready Aim Fire

JOURNAL

Ready Aim Fire

JOURNAL

Ready Aim Fire

Journal

Ready Aim Fire

JOURNAL

Journal